JEZEBEL

Seducing Goddess of War

by

Jonas Clark

Shabazz

JEZEBEL, Seducing Goddess of War
ISBN-10: 1-886885-04-4
ISBN-13: 978-1-886885-04-2

Copyright © 1998 by Jonas Clark
Revised 2004

Published by Spirit of Life Publishing
27 West Hallandale Beach Blvd.
Hallandale Beach, Florida
33009-5437, U.S.A.
(954) 456-4420

www.JonasClark.com

06 07 08 09 ¨ 07 06 05 04 03

ABOUT THE AUTHOR

Jonas Clark is a refreshing voice and a champion in the contemporary church. Jonas served God for more than two decades as a pastor, teacher and evangelist before the Lord called him to his role as an apostle in the end time church.

An evangelist at heart, Jonas travels around the world preaching the Gospel with a bold apostolic anointing. Fortitude and God's grace have taken his ministry into more than 25 countries, where he delivers a message of salvation, healing, deliverance and apostolic reformation. His passion is to win lost souls for Jesus Christ and equip every believer to take the Good News into the harvest fields to fulfill the Great Commission.

Jonas is the founder of The Global Cause Network, an international network of believers and Champion partners united to build a platform for the apostolic voice. He also heads Spirit of Life Ministries, a multi-cultural, non-denominational church in Hallandale Beach, Florida.

Jonas is the publisher of *The Voice* magazine, a media platform for apostolic and prophetic believers.

THIS BOOK IS DEDICATED TO...

All those who are not willing
to tolerate the spirit of Jezebel.

"Notwithstanding I have a few things against thee, because thou sufferest that woman Jezebel..."
(Revelation 2:19-20)

CONTENTS

Jezebel is a master manipulator who uses flattering words and smooth sayings to seduce your soul. She seeks positions of power, influence, favor and authority that allow her to control and advance her evil agenda. Could she be targeting you?

Jezebel likes to isolate her disciples from others in an effort to control their life, and soulishly addict them to her. She does this through mysticism and false prophecy.

By studying the gods of Jezebel, we can pull back the veil of deception and see the true nature of her character. What you find out about these ancient gods — and how they are still working in the world today — may surprise you.

Voice of Healing Prophet William Branham prophesied Jezebel's rise in 1933. Indeed, our generation is a prime target for the greatest deception the world has ever seen, and the Laodicean church will be the victim of that great deception.

The Jezebel spirit is motivated by an insatiable hunger for power and control. The elements of conflict with Jezebel start with the threat and its messenger, and are shaped by our response. Let's face it, Jezebel's threats are serious. Will her menacing messages allow her to control your life or will you disregard her intimidating tactics?

Ahab carries a provoking spirit. He is contentious, argumentative, depressive and hostile toward God's prophets. Ahab is not weak, but he does have insecurities that allow Jezebel to come in and usurp his authority. He will allow Jezebel to use her seducing, warring abilities to do his dirty work.

God called and empowered Jehu, an apostle of war to conquer Jezebel, a goddess of war, and to destroy the house of Ahab.

It takes ruthless faith and militant determination to defeat the Jezebel spirit. Jezebel is not all-powerful. She can be conquered, and God desires to spiritually equip you to be the one to do it.

INTRODUCTION

I met Jezebel some years ago and quickly became intimately acquainted with her wicked ways. Shortly after our brief introduction I found myself being resisted on all fronts, yet I didn't completely understand what that resistance was. You see, Jezebel was yet an unnamed foe. She was at that time a mysterious rival that seemed to know me quite well. It was as if she had studied my strengths and weaknesses as she prepared to wage an all-out war against me.

While I had a revelation of spiritual warfare and binding and loosing, this spiritual war was somehow different and the victory was not swift. The root of the resistance was deeply planted in the spiritual realm. Whoever this unseen rival was, it was not giving up easily. It wasn't even backing down.

I still remember pacing around my backyard in prayer and intercession for hours at a time during those days. What felt like an intense grieving would come upon me regularly and all I could do was cry out to God to unlock the mystery. The grieving intensified and I realized I was in a spiritual war far greater than anything I had experienced in the past. It was a spiritual clash against an unidentified enemy. I can't do justice to the feelings with mere words. Suffice it to say that I knew I was under a vicious spiritual attack. And vicious is still too mild a word. I knew I was in a spiritual war against an especially wicked foe.

This went on for months until one day I heard a minister explaining an experience that was markedly similar to mine. He described the emotions of his soul and even the physical symptoms associated with contending with a spirit called "Jezebel" and he explained that he had to learn how to fight Jezebel so he could launch his ministry.

When I heard him say that, something went off inside of me (an inner witness) and I thought, "That's the same thing that I feel, in my spirit, when I walk around my backyard praying." Once I knew what I was fighting against, I began to study the Word of God for revelation on the wicked wiles of this Jezebel spirit.

If you've picked up this book, then maybe you are feeling the same spiritual clash. When you feel that clash it could be because Jezebel is targeting and attacking you or because the Spirit of God inside of you is opposing the spiritual climate around you. The reason you feel uncomfortable in your spirit sometimes is because your spirit will contend with things unseen (2 Corinthians 4:18).

When God was training me for the ministry He taught me about these things in my backyard so that I would not be ignorant of the devil's devices when He sent me to the nations (2 Corinthians 2:11). It is critical to understand who your enemy is, and for our own protection God will not send us into battle without preparing us. The Holy Spirit Himself taught me how to fight against and conquer Jezebel through prayer and intercession. And once I conquered her, the Lord put it on my heart to write a book to help others break free from this seducing goddess of war.

Brothers and sisters, you must be well prepared to contend with Jezebel, God desires to equip all of His children. I pray that you will glean some spiritual truths and some practical advice that will both help you take Jezebel out of your life and help others become aware of her subtle seductions.

CHAPTER 1

JEZEBEL:
WHO IS THAT WOMAN?

Jezebel is a master manipulator who uses flattering words and smooth sayings to seduce your soul. She seeks positions of power, influence, favor and authority that allow her to control and advance her evil agenda. Could she be targeting you?

Queen Jezebel is first portrayed in the Bible as a wicked monarch who attacked and killed Old Testament prophets of God (1 Kings 18:4). After her timely demise, the name "Jezebel" is not found again in Scripture until the last book of the New Testament (Revelation 2:20). But who is this second woman with the same name? Since dogs ate Queen Jezebel long before Christ was crucified, obviously Scripture is not referring to Queen Jezebel of old, but to another woman who possessed the same evil spirit. With similar characteristics — both were false prophetesses and seductresses — we can discern the same spirit was operating in both women. Today, we call that spirit "Jezebel." We can conclude from our two biblical examples, who lived in different eras, that the same sinister spirit in these women called Jezebel can live on, influence and operate through others today.

In our day, as in the days of the Prophet Elijah who contended directly with Queen Jezebel in Old Testament times, the spirit of Jezebel is on a mission to destroy as many lives as possible. We must learn to identify the spirit of Jezebel operating through people because Jesus made it clear that the Church is not to tolerate her villainous ways. When Jesus spoke to the church at Thyatira in the Book of Revelation, He specifically rebuked it for allowing Jezebel,

> "which calleth herself a prophetess, to teach and seduce" the servants of God (Revelation 2:20).

Yet, why would the Lord be so circumspect about this spirit? Could it be that the Jezebel spirit is one of the most vicious opponents of the born again believer? Could it be that He is concerned about protecting you?

JEZEBEL TODAY

Jezebel can't work her treachery without someone's help. Like a shark, she circles the lives of the vulnerable, prowling for teachable, seducible, controllable disciples to feed from her table (1 Kings 18:19). Jezebel likes to mentor spiritual eunuchs and views them as ornaments who help her manipulate and advance her selfish goals. Jezebel targets those who are rebellious, weak or wounded and she knows how to use deep emotional hurts and wounds to mislead and exploit. Jezebel's aim is to pull people to herself and away from those who can speak truth into their lives. She understands, thoroughly, the power of isolation as she actively searches out the fainthearted and seducible. She seeks to woo those who are being disciplined or corrected by leadership and those living in quiet, yet artful, rebellion. She targets others who resent authority, complain, backbite or gossip. She looks for recruits who will carry her message—those that will tap into her immoral spirit and transfer it to as many others as possible. In the wake of every Jezebel spirit is a life of chaos, confusion and instability that ultimately leads to broken homes, marriages, relationships, churches and utter destruction.

The Jezebel spirit is actively opposing all who live a fervent Christian life. She will come against everyone who carries the voice of the Spirit of God, prophets and prophetic people alike, and those who are discerning and resisting the dark spiritual climates of their cities. Prophesying falsely herself, Jezebel thrives in deceitful spiritual authority — and she knows how to create, flow and operate

> **Jezebel targets those who are rebellious, weak or wounded and she knows how to use deep emotional hurts and wounds to mislead and exploit.**

in counterfeit manifestations of God's Spirit and government. Jezebel is an especially strong enemy of evangelistic ministry. Those who actively share their faith with family and friends are a serious threat and the devil will use the spirit of Jezebel to buffet their effectiveness in ministry.

It is time to expose the methods of the spirit of Jezebel so that our generation can conquer her evil wiles. No longer can we allow her to seduce, teach, prophesy, or to control us or the Church of Jesus Christ. We must rise up with the same conquering spirit of Jehu, who defeated Queen Jezebel, and challenge her on every front. Many have overcome the attacks from the Jezebel spirit after they were armed with the Spirit of Truth, and so can you. Let's look at some common identifiable characteristics of the Jezebel spirit.

THE MASTER SEDUCTRESS

So far we've identified Jezebel as a dangerous spirit who has manifested in multiple generations. But how does the Jezebel spirit operate? How can you tell if you are being victimized, singled out or targeted?

The Jezebel spirit operates initially through seduction. To seduce means, "to cause to stray, to lead away from the truth, to deceive, to wander out of the way, or to lead into error." Jezebel cannot control a person who has not first been seduced. It's only after the seduction that control and manipulation become effective. Jezebel, through the decoy of kind words, drawn by gentle means, entices her victims with vain promises and persuasions designed to enslave her prey in a deceptive net. Jezebel is the master seductress. No one is better at using the allure of flattering words and smooth sayings than her. Beware of vain flattery, smooth prophetic sayings and seducing tears from this spirit.

Jezebel often uses flattering words and smooth sayings to seduce. Her flattering words are insincere compliments spoken to win your favor. There is nothing wrong with a compliment, provided it is offered with the right motive. Vain flattery, however, is one of Jezebel's most seductive weapons. The

> **Jezebel cannot control a person who has not first been seduced.**

Hebrew word for "flattery" is *chalaq,* meaning "to be smooth, to separate, or to divide." Jezebel uses flattery and smooth sayings to win the favor of her victims. A smooth (chalaq) saying is a form of seduction. Smooth sayings could sound something like, "You're so wonderful. No one prophesies like you do. You're so special in God's Kingdom. No one understands you like I do." In this instance, Jezebel uses flattery to feed pride or low self-esteem. After all, she wants you to believe that she is the only one who truly understands your deeply felt needs. Self-serving interests, however, always motivate Jezebel's flattery. She is interested in gaining entrance to your soul. Your soul is your mind, will, intellect, reasoning, imagination and, Jezebel's grandest playground, your emotions. Jezebel is expert at working her seductions in the imaginations and emotions in your soulish realm. Other forms of seduction include the release of controlling words, prophecy, manipulating silence, sexual favors, body language, pouting, false tears, or timely weeping. Each of these is craftily designed to seduce your soul in an effort to get you to come under her control.

JEZEBEL'S MESSENGERS

If Jezebel can't seduce you with flattery and smooth sayings, then she may dispatch her eunuchs (spiritual children) to attack you with prophetic messages laced with fear and discouragement, just as she did with Elijah (1 Kings 19:2). These messengers have the ability to transfer her spirit through words even though she is not personally present.

Once a colleague stopped by the church to pick me up for lunch. He had heard of a new restaurant opening in town with a spectacular ocean view and beautiful boats that passed by as you dined. We both thought it would be a great place to enjoy the South Florida sunshine and discuss some ministry strategies. Just before he picked me up, one of Jezebel's eunuchs called and delivered an unwelcome message from a woman in the congregation who flowed in this controlling spirit. The woman was trying to attain a teaching position in our ministry, but I would not allow it because I knew she carried the spirit of Jezebel. The woman didn't like the fact that she was not going to be allowed to teach and subsequently began to undermine my authority by spewing false accusations to anybody that would listen. The eunuch delivered a message from the woman that said, "I'm going to show him that this isn't over 'til I say it's over."

As I climbed into my friend's car I was inclined to share Jezebel's message with him, too, but stopped short. I recognized that I was about to transfer the same threatening communiqué with which Jezebel had just blindsided me through her faithful eunuch. So after recognizing the enemy's plan to spread the warring assault, I did just the opposite of what that spirit of Jezebel wanted me to do. I began to speak blessings over everyone involved in the situation. I learned a valuable lesson that day. Jezebel wants you to be a carrier of her message. Don't do it. We all have to learn how to respond to Jezebel's message regardless of who she uses to transmit it.

FEAR AND INTIMIDATION

Jezebel doesn't always send a messenger. Sometimes she takes care of business herself. Oftentimes she releases fear at you in order to enforce her control. She might say, "I feel in my spirit like something bad is going to happen to you," or, "I had a

terrible dream last night and I saw you in it."
Jezebel can create an atmosphere of fear and
intimidation. You never quite know how to
take her. Being around her makes you very
uncomfortable. You don't want to talk to
her the way you know you should because
who knows how she's going to respond? She
might suddenly become combative and jump
all over you or she may just leave the room in
a quiet huff. Jezebel can make you scared to
even talk to her. Creating an uncomfortable
atmosphere is a subtle form of control.
Sometimes she might just use the silent
treatment. In India the silent treatment is
recognized as a form of sorcery.

JEZEBEL AND CONFUSION

In addition to fear and intimidation,
Jezebel creates and flows well in atmospheres
of confusion. Spiritual territories where
Jezebel is ruling release strong confusion
that seems to just be "in the spiritual climate."
Some confusion is the direct result of
natural circumstances, but Jezebel releases
a spiritual confusion called witchcraft. This
strong confusion will cause people to forget
the common things that they do every
day. I've watched dedicated servants in
the ministry of helps forget from one week
to the next what they are supposed to do,
even though they have been performing the

same tasks for months. It seems that they can't pull their thoughts together. Others seem confused so much of the time that I sometimes wonder how they function on a daily basis. Could any of this confusion be the direct result of Jezebel's witchcraft?

Some confusion is the direct result of natural circumstances, but Jezebel releases a spiritual confusion called witchcraft.

It's happened to me, too. I'll never forget the time when I was in Europe ministering. I had been invited to preach at a major conference for the first time. While I was preparing for the service, confusion began to hit my mind so hard I literally had a problem remembering my own name. It was unbelievable. That's how strong Jezebel's witchcraft can be. I had never experienced anything like that in my life. Why was I a target? I was scheduled to preach at a particular time and a person with a Jezebel spirit didn't want to see that happen. She didn't want me there because she wanted her "friend" to preach instead. She must have figured that if she could bump me out, then she might be able to break down a door of opportunity for one of her eunuchs.

In order to accomplish her underhanded scheme, Jezebel resorted to her time-tested tactics: false prophecy and witchcraft prayers. She began to prophesy to the conference coordinator that her friend had the Word of the Lord and not me. She told him that he would be missing God by not allowing her friend to bring the Word of the Lord. This is a form of prophetic control that we will discuss in a moment. While her cunning campaign to boot me out of the conference line up was ultimately unsuccessful, her attempts to hinder me were not altogether unfruitful. There was so much confusion released in that conference that I could barely think straight. This woman was praying against me and even gathered several others to agree with her in prayer to remove me from the lineup of speakers. I don't think that everybody praying with her knew what spirit they were tapping into but that didn't matter. This is a common characteristic of Jezebel: She will always contend with those who stand in the way of her personal agenda, even if it means praying witchcraft prayers. It was not her place to determine who was supposed to minister at this conference. She had a hidden personal agenda and caused great confusion throughout that week of meetings. Despite the assignment against me, God was faithful. I preached when scheduled and many were touched powerfully by the Holy

Spirit. Let's look at some other qualities of the Jezebel spirit.

POWER HUNGRY CONTROLLER

Jezebel is a power hungry controller. She'll let you hold a conference as long as she approves of the speakers. She'll let you have a church as long as she can control the flow and set the agenda. She wants to control what songs you sing, how loud you pray, what you preach and with whom you fellowship. That's what she thrives on — controlling power. "No" is an assaulting word to Jezebel. When those in spiritual authority say "no" to her, she is ready for war. Remember, Jezebel is a warring spirit who is always dressed for battle.

JEZEBEL'S PROPHETIC CONTROL

Remember that both Jezebels mentioned in Scripture were false prophetesses. The spirit of Jezebel views personal prophecy as a manipulative means to an ungodly end. Some personal prophecy in the Church today is nothing more than Jezebel's controlling spiritual utterances. Just because the delivery has a spiritual sound or a spiritual punch with it, doesn't mean that it should not be judged, examined thoroughly, and submitted to your leader (1 John 4:1; Hebrews 13:17).

SARAH MEETS JEZEBEL FACE TO FACE

I got an earful from a precious woman named Sarah. Her experience with the Jezebel spirit was textbook. She experienced everything you're reading about and perhaps more. We can learn a lot from these real life experiences... Here is part of her story:

One of Sarah's friends, Becky, invited her to a Bible study. Becky told Sarah that the Lord had revealed to Phyllis, the teacher, that she should join the group. Although Sarah felt uneasy about it, she did not want to be disobedient to the Lord. After all, if the Lord foretold her attendance through this person, then she should by all means go.

Upon Sarah's arrival Phyllis made her feel so special and her teaching seemed to really answer some of Sarah's unasked questions. Phyllis even had a personal prophecy for her. Sarah could not recall a time when she felt so accepted.

Of course, Phyllis claimed that she was a prophetess and that she was in the deliverance ministry at her church. And since Sarah longed to hear directly from the Lord, she accepted Phyllis' super spiritual utterances as coming from the Holy Spirit.

Many times you could hear Phyllis declaring, "God said…"

Phyllis' spiritual life seemed so exciting to Sarah because Phyllis was continually seeing visions and having spiritual-sounding dreams and words of knowledge. Sarah felt that she, too, should be having the same experiences and hungered to learn more of Phyllis' teachings. Oh, how Sarah longed to have the same relationship with the Lord that Phyllis did.

One day during a teaching session Phyllis had a "prophetic word" that no one in the group should ever miss one of her Bible studies again. After that, Sarah felt that if she were to miss even a single Bible study she would be offending the Lord Himself and would be in total rebellion.

DIVIDE AND CONQUER

Jezebel can't tolerate her eunuchs truly getting touched by the Holy Spirit. Nor will she accept anyone else preaching or speaking directly into the life of the person that she is controlling. If you get between Jezebel and the person she's trying to bridle, then you will become the target of her attack. She will do everything she can to destroy your relationship with the one being controlled. She might not physically attack you, but she will try to destroy your reputation and separate you from her student. Jezebel will turn all of her attention on you, and may even set you up for a grand fall in front of her pupil to "prove" to them that you are wrong and she is right.

Ask yourself the following questions to determine if the Jezebel spirit has manipulated you:

> Has someone ever given you a compliment that you knew was insincere?
>
> Do some people tend to flatter you excessively in order to get close to you?
>
> Has someone ever been able to change your mind about a decision that you later regretted making?
>
> Has someone ever threatened you in subtle ways in order to get what they wanted from you?

If you answered yes to any of these questions, then the spirit of Jezebel has probably influenced you.

JEZEBEL'S ATTEMPT
TO HINDER THE HOLY SPIRIT

A young preacher's kid discovered Jezebel operating in his parents' church. What was worse, this Jezebel was on the praise and worship team and attempted to wreak havoc in the sanctuary every chance she got. Listen to Billy's testimony from Michigan:

"I am a 21-year-old minister at my parents' church. My mom and dad are called as a prophetess and apostle. I am called as a prophet myself. I wanted to share with you some of the things I have seen Jezebel do in our church.

At first we did not know it was Jezebel, but as we learned more about her traits we soon realized whom we were dealing with. This spirit moved through people at our church. One in particular was our praise and worship leader. At times when she would lead worship I would hear something screech almost like a bird. At first I thought it was the sound equipment acting up, but it would be so painful I couldn't stand it. She was purposely messing up. When the Holy Spirit would finally fall she would cut us off and butcher the song. She couldn't stand the prophetic voice even when coming through songs. That spirit was seducing and flattering one minute and would cut you the next.

I have seen men on fire for God and when they married a Jezebel they would be emasculated. They would look old and drained as if they had no life. Just recently the Lord told me to name the youth department "Jehu Generation." He said He was going to raise up warriors with a word in their mouth and a sword in their hand that would destroy Jezebel and Baal and not compromise. I had my doubts about the name because I thought it was extreme, but I know that the Lord told me this. Now I see why I am going through attacks. Jezebel doesn't want me to walk in my destiny."

REALM OF INSECURITIES

Have you ever felt insecure? Almost everybody has experienced insecurity about one thing or another. Insecurity is produced by a lack of information, confidence or trust. Jezebel can carry and flow well in atmospheres of fear, frustration and confusion, and has a field day working in the realm of one's insecurities. She knows how to probe your soul, looking for any and every weakness and insecurity you may have. She uses these insecurities to masterfully form soul ties that she will later use to pull you back to her when you begin to turn toward the truth. A soul tie is an emotional bonding between two or more people. Jezebel will never help you overcome your insecurities or build up your self-esteem; she will play on your fears and use them to undermine your feelings of self-worth. She might feed areas of pride that seem to provide a momentary sense of well being, but she won't build true spiritual truth in you that will lead to a balanced Christian life.

PHYLLIS PROBES LIVES
OF HER DISCIPLES

Back to Sarah and Phyllis... Sarah tried to become Phyllis' friend. But the only relationship that Phyllis would allow was centered around her ministering to Sarah. Phyllis would always probe deeply into the lives of those in the group for the most intimate details, but would never open her own heart to the group.

Phyllis had an unusual knack of exposing and talking about the faults of some of the women in the group, supposedly so that they could overcome and have a closer walk with Jesus. She would also hold private prophetic counseling and deliverance sessions. These counseling sessions would continue until tears flowed freely. Phyllis was a master at pouring on the sympathy, even crying herself. This created a kind of emotional bonding between her and the ones being counseled.

Phyllis would always present a relationship with the Lord that seemed so impossible for anyone to obtain, except for her. And Sarah came to believe that Phyllis' emotional stripping of the other women made her spiritually superior to them.

JEZEBEL UNDERMINES YOUR FAITH

Jezebel continually challenges the effectiveness of God's Word in your life in order to keep you emotionally frustrated. Are you distraught or unnerved right now? Have you ever felt exasperated? Jezebel is always distressing her eunuchs, wearing them down and pulling them out of faith. She says things like, "The Holy Spirit didn't really say that to you. That's not what He really meant. God really doesn't want you to do that. God's power can't really flow through your hands. God can't really prophesy through you at a high level. God can't really use you to do that." These types of verbal tactics are designed to undermine your faith, magnify your insecurities, and create new ones.

Can you see the operation of this spirit? Jezebel manifests this way because she wants to use her weapons of witchcraft to fill you with faithless anxieties. Did you ever have Jezebel's messenger come to you saying things like: "God can't use you. Your prayers are never going to be answered. People know

who you are and where you came from."
These are all words that undermine and
plant seeds of doubt and unbelief to weaken
your faith.

TAPPING INTO HURTS & WOUNDS

While your strong points are like walls of
resistance, Jezebel views your weak points
as gateways of control. Jezebel will probe
your soul looking for an emotional weakness
to open a door of hurt and pain that needs to
stay shut. Those doors to your soul can be
emotional hurts and wounds. I have heard
the spirit of Jezebel ask this question many
times, "Is everything all right?" It sounds so
innocent on the surface, doesn't it? But she
wants to know what upsets or emotionally
distrubs you. Don't tell her. Jezebel feeds on
information. That is what she is probing for.
She is walking the aisles of the church today
targeting her prey. Do you realize that many
churches have yet to reach spiritual maturity
because of this spirit? Jezebel keeps things
so stirred up with her sorceries that there is
always a hindering undercurrent.

JEZEBEL THE BACK STABBER

Jezebel fits the quintessential back
stabber profile. She will smile at you, give
you a big hug and kiss, and then turn around

and let you have it when you're not looking. Jezebel is one of the most vicious spirits you will ever encounter. I'll say it again: Jezebel is like a shark, most vicious and dangerous. She circles the lives of others looking for teachable, seducible, controllable disciples to call her own.

JEZEBEL IS SELF-SERVING

Jezebel comes to steal your blessings. Don't make her your prayer partner because she will never get into agreement with you about anything unless it serves her own interests. Jezebel is very dangerous because she can function in three realms: spirit, soul, and flesh. She can tap into the spirit realm and move in the soulish realm. She is a master at seducing you by pulling on your emotions.

THE CLASSIC GOLD DIGGER

You can always recognize Jezebel by her deceitful motivation. Jezebel is a gold digger in the classical sense. A gold digger is a person who, in their personal relations, tries to gain money, gifts, position, influence, status or power. Christians have been told that they are not supposed to judge people. That's not entirely true. I had one religious person criticize me because he felt like I was judging someone. I wasn't; I was merely discerning the spirit behind what someone said. I was looking at the fruit (Matthew 7:20). Ignoring what goes on around us is not Christian service. If someone is manipulative, controlling and self-serving, then we need to pay attention.

JEZEBEL IS POLITICALLY CORRECT

How is this different than be all things to all people?

Jezebel strives to be politically correct. She will change her public opinion about issues based on who's around her at the time. Like a chameleon, Jezebel quickly adapts and adjusts to her surroundings in order to maintain her camouflage.

Once I was in Europe at a ministry meeting discussing some details concerning an upcoming conference. It was very important to all that we allowed the Holy Spirit to dictate the agenda of the next gathering. All of the ministers made a solid, prayerful decision about the upcoming topics and speakers during the meeting, but by the next morning some had changed their minds. The change of mind was completely based on the manipulative lobbying of a Jezebel spirit who talked to each of them individually after the meeting concluded. I could hardly believe the change of heart, but recognized the influence of Jezebel's seducing manipulation at work. I stood against her influence during another meeting the next day by saying, "No. What's wrong with you guys? You make a decision one day and then the next day you change your mind. What's wrong with you?" Whenever someone asks, "What's wrong with you?" it gets everybody's attention. Jezebel's agenda was uncovered and the original plan prevailed. In an attempt to save face, the person who was operating in the Jezebel spirit also agreed that the initial plan was indeed the best plan. That shows you how slick that spirit can be. Jezebel takes political correctness to a whole new level.

Ask yourself the following questions to determine if the Jezebel spirit has targeted you:

> Does someone ask you personal questions in an attempt to uncover your hidden fears or insecurities?

> Does anybody ever reason with you about why God can't do what He has promised you?

> Does someone seem to be trying to stir up old and painful memories in your life?

> Has someone betrayed you after promising to stand by your side?

If you answered yes to any of these questions, then the spirit of Jezebel is probably abusing you.

VYING FOR AUTHORITY

Leaders are one of Jezebel's prime targets because she needs control and influence to advance her devilish agenda. Jezebel relishes power. "Give me, give me, and give me." You see, money is not really the issue, although she also wants the money. It is power and influence that she is really after. She likes to feel that you are her puppet and she pulls the strings. She draws her strength from controlling you. That's why you feel spiritually drained after she battles with you.

It's not just the pastor she's setting her sights on. Jezebel will target any level of church leadership, or even up-and-coming leaders, that she can sink her claws into. In order to seduce you, Jezebel may say things like, "It is a shame that the pastors do not recognize your spiritual gifting. God showed me that you are a prophet and that I am to disciple you. The pastors just do not understand how gifted you are. But I do." Take note that Jezebel feeds her victims with spiritual pride to create an ungodly soul tie and win their confidence. Once her victims are schooling at her table, their ability to discern truth is diminished. Jezebel is very possessive and domineering; she wants to control you.

CONTROLLABLE PASTORS

Jezebel will befriend and support controllable pastors. I once watched grievously as a local church assembly allowed Jezebel to select its pastor. Jezebel was already controlling the pulpit committee and therefore had some influence with the congregation. It was no secret who she was going to vote for because she made sure everyone knew it. Jezebel's seemingly innocent campaign for her choice of pastor had a subtle threat below the surface. While

Jezebel can't work her treachery without someone's help.

she said, "I am voting for Pastor So and So because he has our best interests at heart," the manipulative undertone demanded, "And you better vote for him too, or I'm going to make your life miserable around this church!"

Sadly, this type of thing is happening all over the world. Instead of God assigning His man, the Jezebel spirit uses control, manipulation, intimidation and threats to put in place a leader that will take her tainted advice. Jezebel is looking for controllable pastors who will allow her and her cohorts positions of authority and influence. So instead of God's set-man we often get "hired preachers" who are reduced to nothing more than Jezebel's high-ranking eunuchs. The spirit of Jezebel can make weak men out of strong pastors who refuse to contend with her. That's why leaders must be strong and conquer this spirit. Jezebel can never be ignored.

JEZEBEL GOT OUR PASTOR

I got a letter from a couple in Texas who watched minister after minister fall into adultery via Jezebel's seductions. Their testimony tells of the fear, frustration, sadness and confusion that this couple felt when Jezebel seduced their pastor. Jamie writes:

"Looking back, I can see that a Jezebel spirit controlled our former pastor. All of the time we were under his covering we were confused and depressed. If we shared something with him that God showed us, he would tell us 'That wasn't exactly what God was saying,' then give us his own interpretation.

When I asked him to pray for my healing, I felt condemned if I didn't get healed right away. In fact, most of my physical problems were from the severe stress that I was experiencing under his ministry. I lived in fear and frustration the entire time. It seemed that my joy was nowhere to be found. Because of his controlling ways, he never would release us into ministry. He told me that God was holding me back and not releasing me.

He would tell the whole church that if anyone left the ministry they would be in rebellion and God would not bless them. There were so many things that he would say and do that created confusion when we were around him. We knew something was wrong, but he created fear in everyone and we didn't want to be in rebellion.

He never preached about holiness. He even counseled women alone. His wife was very upset about what was going on. The assistant pastor, the board, and two outside ministers also tried to talk to him about it. But he would never admit he was doing anything wrong and would not accept their counsel.

It wasn't long before he was having an affair with a 17-year-old girl that he was counseling behind those closed doors. When his wife found out about it she left him immediately. We all knew that something was up but he wouldn't tell us what it was. Then, finally, he had to admit to the affair because the girl began to tell everyone about it after they broke up.

After that he left the church and started another one. Then he ended up marrying someone else in his new church. Yes, he continues to pastor today. When he was single for about a year he had many of the women in the church thinking they were going to be his wife. He had such a seducing spirit on him that several women even divorced their husbands in hopes of being with him. It was a terrible experience for everybody.

My husband and I moved to another city after that experience. We needed a lot of healing. We gave up ministry so we could find God again. We are in church and just now getting to a place where we feel like we are getting stronger. We are fasting and praying and seeking the will of God. We want to fulfill the call that God has for us that the spirit of Jezebel stole."

POSSESSIVE AND DOMINEERING

Jezebel is possessive and domineering because she wants to be in control. Whatever measure of authority you have, she wants to use it to serve her purposes. This spirit feels that she's more capable of handling situations than you are. In some cases she may very well be, but if you are in a position of authority, then don't allow her to usurp your position under any circumstances. To usurp means to take power or position by force and without right.

JEZEBEL ATTACKS AUTHORITY

When you won't bow down to her ploys or appoint her a position of leadership, then brace yourself for the attack. I have seen Jezebel attack and contend with many pastors and leaders because she refuses to recognize any spiritual authority other than her own false authority. She may say things like, "Do you know what that elder did at that church? I can't believe it!" or, "Do you know what that deacon said to me? He is way out of line," or, "The pastor is making a terrible mistake. He should have listened to me!"

But it's not just spiritual authority that Jezebel despises. If you listen closely, you'll hear the voice of Jezebel say things like, "I hate those cops; they're always giving people tickets. Why don't they go out there and fight crime?" or, "Did you hear what the president said? He doesn't know what he's talking about." Jezebel is always contending with, verbalizing, attacking and undermining those in positions of authority. There may be times when you're naturally upset with people, but that's not what I'm talking about here. The spirit of Jezebel will contend with any position of leadership from the pastor to the head usher to the clean up ministry to the baseball team captain. She's against anybody that's in authority over her and she refuses to submit.

JEZEBEL: READY FOR WAR

Jezebel cannot bear to submit to true spiritual authority. If you come to her with the Word of the Lord on your lips you had better be ready for war. If you try to bring correction in love, you had better be prepared for an all-out battle. If she perceives that she's not strong enough to take you on, she'll probably just run, but if she senses that you're weak, she'll come at you like a western gunslinger with both barrels blazing.

Jezebel's tactics are no big mystery; they are visible in churches around the world. Jezebel never leaves a church without taking others out with her. Remember, whether you are in church leadership or not, if you are spiritually sensitive and growing in the Lord, you are a potential target. The more open and obedient we are to what the Holy Spirit wants us to do, the more susceptible we are to the warfare tactics of Jezebel.

AUTHORITY THROUGH MANIPULATION

Jezebel exercises her own authority through manipulation. She will try to trick people into obedience. She might tell her children, "If you don't take out the trash, then I won't take you to the store." That is a manipulative form of discipline. We may all have done this, but it's not right. We must be careful not to tap into the spirit of Jezebel. Jezebel is a thief. She robs innocent children of their precious childhood. Her children cannot have fun around her because she is overprotective and smothers them with controlling attention. Because she oversees every single detail of their young lives they can't be themselves around her. This over-protectiveness produces an imbalanced child that doesn't know how to interact with others properly. When Jezebel disciplines her children she is usually too harsh because she will correct them out of the wrong spirit. She is training them in her image and advancing them for her cause rather than God's.

Jezebel uses her authority to manipulate at the office, too. If Jezebel is in authority at the job site, she might say something like, "Annual reviews are coming up next week and you are being considered for promotion. But if you expect a raise then I need you to take on more responsibility around here."

This same Jezebel boss is the one who comes in two hours late, leaves an hour early and expects you to make up the workload. What she really meant was, "If you don't start doing more of my job for me, then you won't get your raise this year." And when Jezebel worms her way into authority at the local church she sets the spiritual and natural agenda. I have seen this spirit control every aspect of the church, from prayer meetings to picnics and from teacher choices to song selections. Remember that everything Jezebel does to help anyone is really not to help at all, but to use people to advance her own self-centered purposes.

JEZEBEL AND CHILDREN

Jezebel knows how to use children to get to you. We know that Jezebel likes to raise up spiritual children that the Word calls eunuchs. Her view, however, of biological children is perverted, too. She says that she loves them but she really doesn't know how to love them. Instead, she uses children as tools and weapons to advance her own selfish motives and to manipulate your heart in order to achieve her goals. Jezebel absolutely abhors accountability and self-discipline. Because she doesn't understand godly discipline and accountability, Jezebel trains her children through manipulation.

Jezebel is not the type to say, "Clean your room because I'm Mom and I told you to do so." Instead, she manipulates her children by saying things like, "If you loved me, then you would clean your room." You see, Jezebel seeks to control and manipulate every circumstance to ensure she gets her own way. She will even bribe her children into obedience by saying, "If you clean your room, I'll take you somewhere special." Can you see her spirit operating?

Our society is raising up a whole generation of children who have been disciplined in an environment of control through manipulation. In some cases it's actually the children who are flowing in the Jezebel spirit. So instead of parents disciplining their children, they allow their children to usurp their parental authority because they don't want to face the contending warfare from their own children.

Ask yourself the following questions to help determine if Jezebel is attempting to usurp your authority:

> Is someone always trying to give you advice that you didn't ask for about important decisions in your life or ministry?

> Does anyone ever offer to handle an uncomfortable situation

for you that is really none of their business?

Have you ever been accused of being controlling because you didn't agree with someone's opinion?

When you bring correction to someone do they challenge your authority and refuse to hear you?

If you answered yes to any of these questions, then you have come in contact with the vicious spirit called Jezebel.

JEZEBEL'S SEDUCTIONS

The apostolic warrior Jehu went into town and told the eunuchs to throw Jezebel from the wall. (A eunuch, in Bible terms, is a man who has been castrated.) When Jezebel heard that Jehu was approaching she began to "paint her face" (2 Kings 9:30). This was a symbol of her seduction. She was putting on her alluring facade in hopes of seducing Jehu and, thereby, saving her life. So we see that Jezebel, if she can, will even seduce you sexually. She will do whatever she needs to do in order to protect her own interests and goals. She will compromise herself — she will even prostitute herself — to maintain her position. But we'll talk more about Jehu and Jezebel's sexual maneuvers later.

GIVING IN TO JEZEBEL

The point is that Jezebel is a master manipulator. If you are married to a woman who operates out of a Jezebel spirit and you are Ahab-inclined, meaning that you allow Jezebel to usurp your authority and to do your dirty work for you, then God is not pleased at all. Like Ahab, many people use Jezebel's warring abilities to do their dirty work for them. They leverage her contending abilities to handle situations that are unpleasant for them. That is not only wrong, but it serves to strengthen the Jezebel spirit that will soon turn her focus on them.

As we close this chapter, it should be noted that the Jezebel spirit is not male or female. Jezebel is not a gender but a spirit. It can flow through anyone and does. In the next chapter we will enter Jezebel's world of mystical visions and spiritual attacks.

SUMMARY
JEZEBEL: WHO IS THAT WOMAN?

Jezebel is a warring, contending spirit who works out of a spirit of controlling manipulation as she attacks those in true spiritual authority.

Jezebel can't work her treachery without the help of somebody.

Jezebel targets those who are rebellious, weak or wounded and she knows how to use deep emotional hurts and wounds to mislead and exploit.

In the wake of every Jezebel spirit is a life of chaos, confusion, and instability that ultimately leads to broken homes, marriages, relationships, churches and utter destruction.

Jezebel cannot control a person who has not first been seduced.

The Hebrew word for "flattery" is *chalaq*, meaning "to be smooth, to separate, or to divide."

Jezebel uses the seduction of flattering words and smooth sayings to gain entrance into one's soulish emotions.

Other forms of seduction include the release of controlling words, prophecy, manipulating silence, sexual favors, body language, pouting, false tears, or timely weeping.

The spirit of Jezebel views personal prophecy as a manipulative means.

Jezebel feeds on information.

Jezebel is a gold digger. A gold digger is a person who, in their personal relations, tries to gain money, gifts, position, influence, status or power.

Like Ahab, many people use Jezebel's warring abilities to do their dirty work for them.

CHAPTER 2

JEZEBEL'S WORLD

Jezebel likes to isolate her disciples from others in
an effort to control their lives, and soullessly addict
them to her. She often does this through mysticism
and false prophecy.

As we begin to explore Jezebel's world, let's review what Jesus said to the church at Thyatira.

"And unto the angel of the church in Thyatira write; these things saith the Son of God, who hath his eyes like unto a flame of fire, and his feet are like fine brass" (Revelation 2:18).

When this Scripture refers to the "angel of the church," it indicates that Jesus was speaking directly to the set leader of the church at Thyatira. The set leader is the one who is delegated by heaven and given spiritual oversight of a particular church. On the surface of the Scripture it seems the church at Thyatira is a commendable, wonderful ministry. Jesus said, "I know thy works, and charity, and service, and faith, and thy patience, and thy works; and the last to be more than the first." But then He says,

> "Notwithstanding I have a few things against thee, because thou sufferest that woman Jezebel, which calleth herself a prophetess, to teach and to seduce my servants to commit fornication, and to eat things sacrificed unto idols" (Revelation 2:19-20).

This church demonstrates strong works, love, and is full of committed, dedicated people of faith and patience. The ministry seems to be thriving, but God still holds them accountable for allowing the operations of Jezebel in their midst. First, God points out that they tolerate Jezebel, meaning they know she is in their midst but allow her to operate anyway. Secondly, we learn that Jezebel appears to be prophetic in operation. And finally, God points out Jezebel's desire to teach and to seduce the children of

God, thereby leading them into some sort of idolatrous condition. Let's examine the motives behind Jezebel's yearning to teach and prophesy.

JEZEBEL LIKES TO TEACH

A Bible teacher is one who explains and expounds on the Word of God. Jezebel likes to draw people to herself so she can teach them her own perverted views, doctrines and Scripture interpretation. I have watched those with the Jezebel spirit maintain a running commentary during the church service, explaining to her disciples her skewed interpretation of what the man of God is preaching.

Jezebel will say things like, "Well, this is the way I picked it up in the spirit. This is what I got a witness to. This is how I believe it. This is what the pastor really meant. Oh, you don't need to listen to that— just listen to me." The next phase of her wicked scheme is to pull potential students closer to her through control. "Let's not go to that church," she'll suggest. "They are old-fashioned. Let's go to this other church instead." The next thing you know Jezebel has you hopping from one church to the next so that you never get planted anywhere and nobody but she can speak into your life.

JEZEBEL'S ENTRANCE

When Jezebel enters a church she will immediately begin to seek out open teaching positions. I can still remember when we started Spirit of Life Ministries church in Hallandale Beach, Fla. You wouldn't believe how many Jezebels approached my wife and I volunteering to serve as teachers.

Jezebel likes to draw people to herself so she can teach them her own perverted views, doctrines and Scripture interpretation.

If you will not let them teach, then they usually attempt to breed division by flinging unfounded accusations against you. Most of them will eventually leave the church looking for positions of influence in another local body.

For example, when I politely refused to allow a middle-aged woman who carried the Jezebel spirit to teach a leadership workshop at our church she publicly accused me of having a "man-made church and not a God-made church" and promptly left the ministry in a huff. It's ironically humorous that just a few days earlier she privately told me how wonderful I was and how blessed she was to be in a "Spirit-led" church. Jezebel uses seductive flattery, remember? The woman's compliment was exposed as the insincere manipulation that it was.

JEZEBEL'S MYSTICAL VISIONS

As we learn from the church at Thyatira, Jezebel calls herself a prophetess. Many people carrying the Jezebel spirit have an air of spiritualism about them, meaning that they are spiritually sensitive with a twist of mysticism. When I use the terms "mysticism" or "mystical" I am describing a manifestation that is spiritual in nature but not from the Spirit of God. Jezebel's prophecies sound spiritual and may be delivered in a way that seems godly, but are not easily understood because they are often riddled with indistinguishable mysticism. Without true spiritual discernment one can be easily fooled by Jezebel's mystical prophecies — and many are.

When Jezebel releases a personal prophecy it is commonly accompanied by some element of fear. Prophecy is supposed to edify, comfort and exhort — not intimidate, curse, or release fear (1 Corinthians 14). Jezebel may say something like, "God showed me that your son has an enormous call on his life, but you better guard him because there is a dark force being launched against him in the distant future." Guard him? Of course you would guard your son. Of course the devil will oppose him. But we don't need to live in a state of fear wondering when the spiritual bogie man is going to jump out of the darkness and attack our children.

I've heard many a Jezebel try to interpret what I call controlling or mystical visions. These visions are generally ambiguous. Either no one could really understand them at all or you could interpret them 50 different ways. I am not against prophecy. I value what God is doing through true prophetic ministry today. It is vital to the Church. But it is also crucial that the source of the prophetic word be discerned. What I do oppose is the prophetic operations of Jezebel because they present our God as a mystical God who is not easily understood and who is difficult to interpret. Difficult-to-interpret, mystical visions and prophecies are Jezebel's playground because she is left alone to offer an interpretation that advances her foul agenda.

The Word of God declares that the Holy Spirit speaks "expressly" (1 Timothy 4:1). This means that God is perfectly capable of making Himself very clear and does not muddy His prophetic word in mystical ambiguous sayings. Our God is not clouded in mysticism. He doesn't need help from spiritist Jezebels for you to understand Him.

JEZEBEL'S HAREM OF FOLLOWERS

A Wyoming couple watched as Jezebel used her spiritual children and her husband Ahab to further her wicked cause by sending evil messages. Read this couple's experience with the Jezebel spirit:

I have come into contact with a Jezebel spirit. This spirit is very dominant in the Spirit-filled churches in the state of Wyoming. It is a territorial spirit here. I know of a town in western Wyoming where Jezebel shut down eight Spirit-filled churches.

You talk about Jezebel having spiritual children. I have always seen it as a harem of followers. I also have seen this spirit rob anointing off of unsuspecting ministers, evangelists and other people who were called of God. She doesn't do it directly, but she uses her harem of followers to send messages to each of the called ones that causes them to leave in strife.

Jezebel also has an Ahab in the background somewhere. He usually is not directly involved in church matters, so she can tell him whatever she wants him to know. She purposes to keep him out of any church involvement. She uses Ahab as a false head of the household.

I also have found those with a Jezebel spirit to be very versed in the Word of God, and they like to be called the prophetess of the church. But if there is an apostolic anointing on the pastor, then she will not come at him directly. Instead, she will use her powers of control and manipulation over the local church body to create sedition. Toward anyone else she is bold enough to face them directly.

This spirit doesn't like to give prophecy in the church itself, but likes to go around to different members in the body and speak her cunning words. If she does have a word to give it will have a lot of, "I think God told me, I believe God said, etc.," spread throughout.

It was a tough lesson to learn about this spirit, but now God has blessed me to see it in many shapes and forms. You would be surprised at how many of these Jezebel spirits like to show up at women's retreats, women's rallies and conventions.

CREATING PROPHETIC DIRECTION

Jezebel likes to isolate her disciples from others that can speak truth into their lives. If you allow her to draw you away from your trusted friends, then before you know it you may find yourself emotionally dependent upon her for everything. You will soon become soulishly addicted to her because she keeps you coming back for more. Some people are so desperate for direction and answers that they will chase her for personal prophetic utterances just like lost souls rack up huge bills calling telephone psychics. Remember, Jezebel calls herself a prophetess. And, of course, she is very prophetic. That means that she can flow in false personal prophecy. <u>She can tap into a counterfeit prophetic flow as she picks up on familiar spirits.</u>

Jezebel views personal prophecy as a tool to control you and to elevate her spiritualism.

Jezebel is devious. She may only prophesy a short smooth saying designed to hook you and entice you to chase her for the next prophetic word. Then next week she may give you another short prophetic utterance in an underhanded attempt to addict you to her false prophetic insight. Alternatively, she may set herself out as one with a gift of interpretation to get you coming to her for prophetic insight into your puzzling dreams for which she will invent a meaning. Or perhaps worse, she will falsely interpret your God-given dreams, twisting them to serve her purposes.

So what is Jezebel's motive? She does not want you to pursue God for direction. She wants you to cling to her instead. This great chase is one of her control tactics. Jezebel views personal prophecy as a tool to control you and to elevate her spiritualism. It is important to understand that most people operating in this flow do not recognize the Jezebel influence on their activities. But it is critical that you do. Jezebel views "super spiritualism" as a sign of having arrived at some high ranking spiritual level. Let me say right here that the more spiritual you are the more relatable you should be.

PHYLLIS ISOLATES HER SPIRITUAL CHILDREN

Sarah was getting deeper and deeper into Phyllis' control game. Little did she know that one day Phyllis would announce to the group that they should not allow anyone else to counsel them or pray with them. Sarah said that she had been talking with her pastor and asked if that applied to him, too. Phyllis responded by saying that it was impossible for her pastor to know her like she did and that he was not walking in the same place spiritually as she was, so it wasn't a good idea.

Sarah had a close friend at another church that, from time to time, would encourage her in the Word. Phyllis knew this and one day she called Sarah really early in the morning to warn her to avoid that friend. Phyllis said she had a dream that Sarah would be in grave danger if she continued the relationship.

By this time, Sarah had heard Phyllis give out these types of warnings before, and she was afraid not to take it to heart. Once another from the group left and Sarah heard Phyllis question whether the girl would keep her deliverance after leaving.

Phyllis had a way of causing Sarah and the others to feel a great need for more prophetic revelation from her and her alone. And Phyllis was really good at using the Scriptures to support her "new revelations." It seemed as though no one could interpret the Bible like she could. Phyllis spent a lot of time telling those in the group about her spiritual accomplishments. It appeared that everything that she did was so perfect.

JEZEBEL'S TIES THAT BIND

The Jezebel spirit likes to bind you to her so she can ultimately steal your liberty. She will allow you to be spiritual, but she wants you to go out into the realm of the spirit with her instead of with God so that she can keep tabs on you.

There are a lot of people who call themselves Christians that are operating in a spirit realm outside of God. I cannot emphasize this point enough: The spirit of Jezebel views prophecy as a means to control. Did you know that some of the words of knowledge and words of wisdom that are prophesied in the Church today are nothing more than charismatic fortunetelling or Jezebel's spiritualism? But because the delivery has a spiritual punch to it, people

Prophecy in exchange for money is merchandising the gift of God.

sometimes think it is coming from God. The truth is that even the devil can prophesy truth. The damsel possessed with a spirit of divination said of the apostles,

> "These men are the servants of the most high God, which show unto us the way of salvation" (Acts 16:17).

JEZEBEL GOES HOLLYWOOD

Many times when Jezebel emerges from her covert activities and into the public eye she "goes Hollywood." Hollywood Christians are those that won't speak at your conference unless you pick them up in a limousine. God forbid if they had to ride in the car with you instead. God forbid if there's no five-star hotel in your town. And there's no way they would ever go to a third world country to minister to those who have nothing to return but their heartfelt appreciation — that's not good enough for them. They prefer the Hollywood Christianity scene. The next step for these Hollywood Jezebels is to merchandise what appear to be gifts of the Holy Spirit.

MERCHANDISING THE GIFTS OF GOD

Jezebel will use prophetic manipulation to steal your money. If someone prophesies over you to get into your pocket book, then you need to get your purse and go home. Leave the meeting. Run from there and don't ever go back. Then bind every word spoken over you in Jesus' name. Prophecy in exchange for money is merchandising the gift of God. It is the result of Ashtoreth's and Baal's demonic influence. We will look closer at these spirits in another chapter.

God doesn't manipulate His people. That is the control of the Jezebel spirit. God doesn't prophesy over you to coerce you. That's Jezebel's witchcraft. God doesn't prophesy over you to get into your pocket book. That's merchandising — and it's a sin! Whenever God prophesies over you, His purpose is to bring you closer to Him and His design for your life.

JEZEBEL INTRODUCES IDOLATRY

Jesus also said of Jezebel's activity,

> "And to seduce my servants to commit fornication, and to eat things sacrificed unto idols" (Revelation 2:20).

Jezebel will pull you out of a stable church to chase after things that are not real or to follow after the current empty Christian fads. She and her disciples will actively pursue every "new revelation" that is introduced into the Church, despite its credibility, or lack thereof. Since Jezebel is not after spiritual stability, but rather super spiritualism, she leads her disciples from place to place chasing the rising superstars of Christianity, thus hindering anyone from being planted in a particular church. Jezebel has a tendency to exalt people and personalities over Jesus. To her the Christian personality has the fame that she so desperately covets. Jezebel gets bored with "average" ministry because the messengers may not "look" the part. They don't sing the same songs, they don't preach the same way, they don't deliver prophecies with the same flare, or display the same glitter. Be careful not to get carnally addicted to Hollywood personalities rather than the voice of God, which can come through any of His servants.

PHYLLIS DRAGS DISCIPLES
FROM CHURCH TO CHURCH

After some months, Sarah began to notice that Phyllis never really stayed at any particular church very long. There were lots of times when she would ask the group to attend a new church with her or accompany her revival meetings around town. After the meetings, Phyllis would explain to the group what everything meant for them.

When Phyllis did go to church she would let others know about her dreams and visions concerning that church. She also looked for those that she felt needed to attend her Bible study while church hopping. Phyllis seemed to always receive prophetic words and dreams about the pastors and church leaders. Sarah never could understand why the pastors never received Phyllis's prophetic warnings about the impending danger and sin in the churches. If the pastors would not receive Phyllis, then she would get really angry and tell the others to stay away from them.

One time Sarah remembered being in a church with Phyllis and the pastor seemed to really want to talk with Phyllis. He seemed to really have a heart for her. That's when Phyllis began to stay at home and avoid the pastor. She told Sarah that she needed to spend more time alone in prayer with the Lord.

Ask yourself the following questions to determine if Jezebel is trying to deceive you with her false prophetic flow and teaching:

Is someone's teaching contradicting what's coming forth from the pulpit of your church?

Does a prophecy serve God's purposes or the deliverer's purposes?

Is someone undermining the credibility of a bona fide prophetic word released into your life?

Is someone trying to draw you to themselves with their ability to tap into the spirit realm for guidance?

Has someone offered you a prophetic word in exchange for money?

If you answered yes to any of these questions, then you may have fallen prey to false prophetic operations.

JEZEBEL'S TERRITORIAL ATTACKS

I remember receiving a fax from an evangelist that read: "I'm preaching in a church tonight that has more witchcraft in it than any church I've ever been in." "Witchcraft in the church" I thought? The fax continued, "You know what? They can't even sit still long enough to grab their minds and listen to me. Please pray for me tonight. I feel like I'm falling asleep, too."

There was indeed a spirit of witchcraft attacking the people in that church and they could not stay awake during the services. The force was so strong that it was even hitting the evangelist. Her faxed message went on to say, "There are five churches coming together for revival and I need help to bind this witchcraft in prayer. I can't even talk to them about it because they don't understand what witchcraft is. But you know, so please ask your church to pray with me because this thing is trying to take me out before I can get in there to break it open."

Why so much resistance? Because this evangelist had spiritual discernment, and the closer you get to God the more you'll be able to understand Jezebel's territorial attacks. Little did she know at the time that Jezebel in the church was the source of the witchcraft.

JEZEBEL IN THE MARKETPLACE

Jezebel can also wheedle her way into your business life. Be wise about the companies that you do business with. Listen carefully when someone calls you. Is there a Jezebel spirit operating in those who call? Who pays the bills? If a Jezebel spirit is paying the bills at a company that you want to do business with, then you have all the more reason to be cautious. Jezebel will try to control you and she'll do it by saying something like, "I am going to write this check out to you — but..."

While it's always better to remain debt free, if you must borrow money from the bank then be careful about who is in charge. If a Jezebel spirit is in authority, then go elsewhere because she has the power to make your life miserable. You had better know whom you are dealing with because Jezebel is a vicious, brutal spirit. Don't ever yoke yourself up with someone carrying a Jezebel spirit. He or she will make your life so miserable that you will wish that you were in heaven.

JEZEBEL RELATIVES STIR UP STRIFE

I'm not the only one who has seen Jezebel try to break up the family. Many others have written me to share similar experiences. Here's the story of a woman in Oregon who continues to battle the Jezebel spirit:

"I have battled against a Jezebel spirit working through relatives for several years. Both my husband and I have been intimidated, deceived, torn apart and wounded by this spirit.

There are certain relatives on both my husband's and my side of the family that try to bring division, disunity, control, witchcraft and intimidation into our family and in our marriage. We have confronted our relatives about their behaviors, but they have refused to repent or change. My husband and I have come into agreement about some of these relatives, and we have separated ourselves from them. So far it has been the only way we have been able to keep their controlling influences away from us.

My husband comes out of a family with strong Jezebel influences and is still coming out of bondage himself. It has not always been easy for him to stand with me. I have battled successfully for his soul on this issue, even though the enemy has tried to split us up several times. I have also been getting my own life cleansed and healed so that I don't have any open doors in my life.

Sometimes it is hard to get people to realize how cunning, dangerous, and persistent this spirit is. I feel like people think I am just exaggerating and I know that I am not. There is a lot of complacency about this spirit and I am not called to compromise. Jesus tells us in Revelation not to tolerate Jezebel.

In the meantime I need victory from the attacks against my family. This spirit is cunning and dangerous. I have been so intimidated by this spirit and wounded that I am just not going to put up with it anymore!"

JEZEBEL WANTS TO RULE YOUR HOUSE

The spirit of Jezebel won't stop at your place of work. She will even try to rule your roost if you let her. Have you ever had someone try to rule in your own home? Perhaps a relative with a Jezebel spirit? I have and I can tell you that it's not at all pleasant. A person flowing in this rebellious spirit once forced me into a head-on conflict in both the spiritual and natural realms when she tried to separate my wife and me with malicious gossip and sedition. Well, this Jezebel found herself in a war that she wasn't expecting. I simply picked up her bags, threw them out on the front porch and locked her out of the house. Jezebel is not afraid to put you in situations that you don't want to be in, as evidenced by this experience. But as uncomfortable as that was for everyone involved, I had no choice but to exercise my authority as head of the household — or hand it over to Jezebel. Even though I loved the person who the spirit was operating through, I had to separate the spirit from the person and come against the spirit to put an end to her attempts to rule over me, my family and my house. We must have the spiritual strength and fortitude to do what is necessary to disallow her from usurping any authority on the home front. We must never let Jezebel disrupt our world. When we remove the veil of this controlling, manipulative spirit we can see it more clearly and know how to fight back.

JEZEBEL IN THE DEPTHS OF SATAN

Then Jesus said,

> "But unto you I say, and unto the rest in Thyatira, as many as have not this doctrine, and which have not known the depths of Satan, as they speak; I will put upon you none other burden" (Revelation 2:24).

Jezebel works out of the depths of Satan's demonic power. Jesus said, "I will put no other burden on you other than this one." If you don't know anything else about spiritual warfare, at least know this: You can't afford to tolerate Jezebel in your midst. That's what God is saying in these Scriptures. Don't let her function and operate in your midst. Don't let her flow in your church or place of work. Don't let her work in your household. Don't let her teach anyone you know. Don't let her usurp your authority. We must break the power of her influence by removing her from service.

Ask yourself the following questions to determine if you have faced Jezebel at work or on the home front:

> Do you feel unduly obligated to a banker or a boss because they seem to have a stake in your financial destiny?

> Do your promotions and raises come with conditions that only serve to help your boss and not necessarily the company?

> Has a visitor in your home stirred up trouble in your family?

Have you been forced to confront family members who use gossip and false accusations to bring strife and division into your home?

If you answered yes to these questions, then you have probably had lunch — or dinner — with Jezebel.

THE NATIONS OPEN TO THE OVERCOMER

Finally, Jesus says to the church at Thyatira,

> "But that which ye have already hold fast till I come. And he that overcometh, and keepeth my works unto the end, to him will I give power over the nations" (Revelation 2:25-26).

If you look up the Greek word for "overcometh," you will find that it means "to carry off the victory." This is God's plan for you. It also means "to conquer that which challenges the Word of God in your life." Now let's read the verse like this: "To him that conquers the spirit of Jezebel and keeps My works unto the end, to him will I give power over nations." Notice that Jesus makes a promise to "those that overcome" the spirit of Jezebel. Jesus said when we overcome we will have "power over the nations." That means that God will advance your life and ministry beyond where it is today. Do you have a ministry? If you are a born again believer you do. Do you want to be more effective in your ministry so you can help to establish the Kingdom of God? Then you'd better learn how to overcome the spirit of Jezebel. If not, then you will never be very

You will have no ministry to the nations until you learn how to conquer Jezebel.

effective — Jezebel will make sure of that. Every effective minister that I have ever met has had to contend with and conquer the spirit of Jezebel, and you will too.

On the other hand, you will have no ministry to the nations until you learn how to conquer Jezebel, her false prophets and her spiritual eunuchs who attack your ministry. God will not be able to use you on a national or international level until you are able to overcome this wicked spirit. God needs conquerors. You can never move out of your local neighborhood, in fullness, until you learn how to subdue the spirit of Jezebel. Your spiritual condition and your spiritual life will not grow properly until you learn how to defeat the spirit of Jezebel.

The Jezebel spirit will take you out if you don't conquer her first. Jezebel will attempt to void all of your spiritual gifts through her witchcraft maneuvers. She won't let you flow, operate or function in your calling. When you prophesy, for example, she'll be pulling people out of the church right in the middle of your prophetic utterance. She'll grab everybody and turn them around, have them looking unto her as their leader while provoking them to attack you. The good news is that you can win every time!

HOW TO FUNCTION IN JEZEBEL'S TERRITORY

If you are going to live in victory you must understand how to function in the territory God has assigned you. If you're going to be an effective minister, then you really have to flow in spiritual discernment. So if you're falling asleep right before you are supposed to minister, or when you need to prepare your heart, then there's something wrong. You either have not received enough rest, or you are under spiritual attack. When you walk into a church you'd better be able to discern what's working there and be able to hit it in intercessory prayer. Amen?

Sometimes when I walk around my back yard something goes off inside of me, an inner witness, that says, "Time for battle!" If that happens to you, then you had better rise up and fight in the spirit of prayer. Submit yourself to God, resist the devil and he will flee. Don't go to bed or turn on the TV when you are supposed to be praying or you will give the enemy a chance to get an advantage over you.

South Florida, like many regions throughout the world, has a hard spiritual climate. People who are not used to the spiritual resistance we encounter or fail to discern the spiritual war we battle often wind up shutting down when they feel the unseen struggle with the principalities and powers that live in the heavens here. They shut down their spirits and feed their flesh with ice cream or whatever else gratifies them at the moment. Or they shut off their spiritual discernment, ignore the warfare coming against them, and turn on the TV, rent a movie or just go to sleep instead. So while their spirit is blaring "pray!" they either don't have the discernment to recognize the battle cry or they are weary from the fight and choose to seek relief in the natural realm. Unfortunately, both choices cause them to remain ineffective carnal Christians.

TO STEAL, KILL AND DESTROY

Many times you can pick up, in the realm of the spirit, the attack of Jezebel as it comes to steal, kill, and destroy. She'll target you with a fearful message. The message might be, "God's not going to provide your needs at all." Then instead of recognizing her lying voice for what it is, entering into prayer, fasting, travail or even a groaning, you'll spiritually "check out" and look for relief in a bag of potato chips or go home and go to bed. You must understand that Jezebel can attack you in the spirit realm whether she is standing physically in the room with you or not. While Jezebel often operates through a person, we are speaking about a spirit here and not flesh and blood (Ephesians 6:12). Don't underestimate this wicked foe.

In the following chapter we will explore the gods of Jezebel. By studying them we can see the true nature of Jezebel's character.

SUMMARY
JEZEBEL'S WORLD

Jezebel likes to draw people to herself so she can teach them her own perverted views, doctrines and Scripture interpretation.

When Jezebel enters a church she will look for open teaching positions.

Jezebel's prophecies sound spiritual and may be delivered in a way that seems godly, but are not easily understood because they are often riddled with indistinguishable mysticism.

Prophecy is supposed to edify, comfort and exhort — not intimidate, curse, or release fear (1 Corinthians 14).

Difficult-to-interpret, mystical visions and prophecies are Jezebel's playground because she is left alone to do the interpreting.

Jezebel views "super spiritualism" as a sign of having arrived at some high ranking spiritual level.

Prophecy in exchange for money is merchandising the gift of God.

Jezebel will attempt to void all of your spiritual gifts through her witchcraft maneuvers.

Jezebel can attack you in the spirit realm whether she is standing physically in the room with you or not.

CHAPTER 3

THE GODS OF JEZEBEL

*By studying the gods of Jezebel, we can pull back
the veil of deception and see the true nature of her
character. What you find out about these ancient gods
— and how they are still working in the world today
— may surprise you.*

Now that you've been introduced to
our sinister seductress and her
wicked ways, let's take a look at the
gods of Jezebel and her husband Ahab. By
studying these ungodly gods we can get a
better understanding of the latent forces of
our diabolical duo — and the intensity of the
battle Prophet Elijah and Jehu faced when
they confronted them. Let's pull back the
veil and discern the motivations of the gods
that influenced these maniacal monarchs.
As you read the following pages you will
discover that Baal, Dagon and Ashtoreth

are intimately connected to the warring Jezebel spirit.

THE SIDONIAN GODS

We need look no further than the marriage of Jezebel and Ahab to trace the origin of the Jezebel spirit. When Ahab's father, Omri, presided as king of Israel he introduced a policy of befriending other nations and often used marriage between his family members and those of other countries to promote mutual good will. This strategy begot various alliances and served to strengthen Omri's kingship. Omri sealed an alliance with Phoenicia (current day coastal Lebanon) through the marriage of his son Ahab to Jezebel. Jezebel was the daughter of Ethbaal, the king of the Sidonians (1 King 16:31). This seems all well and good until you see what became of it. The Sidonians worshipped two gods: Baal and Ashtoreth. What makes this so interesting is that Ethbaal was not only a king, he was also the high priest of a goddess. That goddess' name was Ashtoreth. Jezebel, therefore, was raised serving two pagan deities.

Apparently Jezebel didn't waste anytime introducing the forbidden worship of Baal and Ashtoreth to her newlywed King Ahab. Soon after their marriage Ahab built a temple first to Baal and later to Ashtoreth as an expression of his love for his bride. We are going to discover as we study this out that it is really not Jezebel wreaking havoc on the world, but rather the goddess Ashtoreth.

Ashtoreth is identified with several different names throughout history worth noting, including "bride of heaven," "goddess of holiness," and "goddess of good fortune." She was also known as the "queen of heaven," a title Catholics use for Mary, Jesus' mother. Ashtoreth is also called by several other names, including Astarte, Ishtar, Ashtart, Asherah and Aphrodite. Whatever you prefer to call her, Ashtoreth and the spirit of Jezebel are one and the same.

BAAL: THE SIDONIAN MALE DEITY

Let's not forget Baal, the primary Sidonian male deity. Understanding Baal is just as important to discerning the Jezebel spirit because history states that Ashtoreth (A.K.A. the Jezebel spirit) was the wife of Baal. This is significant as marriage marks a covenant relationship between two parties that compliment and complete one another. Jezebel, therefore, will manifest many traits of the Baal spirit. Knowing the attributes of both Baal and Ashtoreth gives us deeper insight into the operations of the Jezebel spirit.

Both Ahab and Jezebel were Ashtoreth and Baal worshipers. Remember, Baal was the principal male god of the Phoenicians (Sidonians), where Ashtoreth was the principal female god. Ahab introduced idol worship into Israel by erecting a temple for Baal in Samaria where forbidden ceremonies were enacted (1 Kings 16:32). The Baal god can be traced as far back in biblical history as the Exodus of the Israelites from Egypt. Baal, depicted as a calf or bull, was the very same deity the children of Israel worshipped in the wilderness. You'll recall when Moses climbed up the mountain to receive the 10 commandments from God in Exodus 32. Before Moses could get down the mountain and back to the camp with the stone tablets, Aaron had already submitted to the defecting Israelites' desire to fashion another god, saying,

> "Up, make us gods, which shall
> go before us; as for this Moses,
> the man that brought us up out
> of the land of Egypt, we know
> not what is become of him"
> (Exodus 32:1).

With their leader gone, the spirit of Baal was successful at pulling God's people away from Him and into blatant idolatry. The Israelites gathered their golden jewelry (spoils of their deliverance from Egypt) put them into a blazing fire, and out came a molten calf. This golden calf, fashioned by demonic powers, was referred to as Baal. After the children of Israel pulled the idol from the fire, they built an altar to it where they danced, offered sacrifices and committed illicit acts of sexual immorality (Exodus 32:8). When Moses returned he was so furious at the sight of such shameless idolatry that he broke the stone tablets containing Jehovah's covenant — a prophetic sign that the people had broken their covenant with God (Exodus 32:19).

Jezebel will manifest many traits of the Baal spirit.

The Bible goes on to say that the idol worshippers were uncovered. This nakedness was also symbolic; revealing that the Israelites no longer had the covering or the protection of Jehovah God (Exodus 32:25). God was so angry at their ungratefulness and rebellion that He wanted to completely blot them out of His salvation plan and destroy them (Exodus 32:10). That's when Moses went before God in prayer and intercession, crying out to Him to remember His name and His covenant with Abraham,

Isaac and Jacob. God responded to Moses' supplications saying,

> "I will only blot out from My book those that sin against Me" (Exodus 32:32-33).

Not only did God break His covenant with them, but the Bible also says that His presence left the people. This is evidenced by the Tabernacle being placed outside the camp. The glory of the Lord was no longer in the midst of the Church. The people had to go outside the camp to find Him because He would not share His presence with idol worshippers. Worship of the Baal spirit separated the Israelites from Jehovah.

Even though Moses ordered the deaths of many who worshipped Baal that day, abominable acts would still take place throughout the camp. The spirit of Baal was fast at work deceiving the rebellious. Fed up, Moses asked the people a life and death question:

> "Who is on the Lord's side? Let him come unto me" (Exodus 32:26).

He gave them one final opportunity to choose whom they would serve — Jehovah their deliverer or Baal their deceiver. Like so many lost souls today, thousands made the wrong decision. Many turned their back on Jehovah and chose the deception of Baal and in doing so chose death. Moses sent Levites, Jehovah's priests, into the camp to slay 3,000 men who refused to repent for betraying God with their forbidden idolatry (Exodus 32:28).

BAAL AND PROPHETIC DIVINATION

Scripture has more to say about Baal. One of Baal's most striking characteristics is his ability to prophesy. Baal is a god of prophetic divination. We learn that Baal was prophetic through the famous Mount Carmel showdown between Jehovah's Prophet Elijah and the 450 prophets of Baal who ate at Jezebel's table. When Elijah confronted the prophets of Baal we learn something amazing. Scripture teaches us that they expected Baal to speak through them.

> "And they cried aloud, and cut themselves after their manner with knives and lancets, till the blood gushed out upon them. And it came to pass, when midday was past, and they prophesied until the time of the offering of the evening sacrifice, that there was neither voice,

nor any to answer, nor any that
regarded" (1 Kings 18:28-29).

These prophets of Baal, we learn, were
trained by Queen Jezebel to tap into this
prophetic spirit of divination.

The "calf god" Baal has many aliases.
Three of his more common titles are "exalted
lord of the earth," "rider of the clouds,"
and, most revealing, "lord of the city." It
is obvious that many cities are not open
to the Gospel of Jesus Christ. Could it be
possible that some of these cities are under
the territorial rule of the Baal spirit? Baal's
title, "lord of the city," certainly reflects his
serpentine assignment.

DAGON: EROTIC LUST

History also teaches that Baal was the
son of another god named "Dagon." Dagon
was known as the "god of fertility" or, more
precisely, erotic lust. Dagon was a warrior
who fought against many enemies that
opposed his rule, eventually died and was
born again. Does the resurrection theme
sound familiar? Dagon, like his son Baal,
was also known as "rider of the clouds,"
and "god of the heavens" (meaning god of
the horoscope). He was the deity of rain and
storms and was associated with the goddess
called "little lightning," "daughter of light,"

"little dew," or "little earth." Could this explain the close association of "Mother Earth" with modern environmental activist movements? Dagon was believed to be transported from place to place through fantasy. (We will talk more about fantasy when we discuss Ahab in chapter six.) Dagon's consort was Ashtoreth, also known as the "wife of Baal." Ashtoreth's connection with Dagon the warrior god of erotic lust is quite revelatory. It shows us where Jezebel (Ashtoreth) gets her seducing and warring attributes.

Dagon was also the god of the Philistines who took the ark of God and placed it in the temple of this false god. Dagon's fate, in the presence of Jehovah, is surprisingly similar to that of Queen Jezebel (2 Kings 9:35). Scripture says,

> "Dagon was fallen upon his face
> to the ground before the ark of
> the Lord; and the head of Dagon
> and the palms of his hands
> were cut off upon the threshold;
> only the stump of Dagon was
> left to him (1 Samuel 5:4).

The sexual immorality, including homosexuality, of Dagon followers could explain why Jehovah plagued them with hemorrhoids.

ASHTORETH: SEX AND WAR

Now let's look at the goddess Ashtoreth a little more closely. Ashtoreth is the "goddess of sex" and the "goddess of war." She was a female deity characterized by gross sensuality and lasciviousness. The worship given Ashtoreth was often accompanied with human sacrifice, the burning of incense, violent and ecstatic exercises, ceremonial acts of bowing and kissing, sexual rites, and preparing of sacred mystic cakes. These

> **There is a strong connection between homosexuality and the Ashtoreth spirit.**

mystic cakes were loaves molded in the image of Ashtoreth and were referred to as "the bread of life."

You can see Ashtoreth's influence throughout the world today. Aphrodite, for example, is the primary object of the feminist goddess movement. Ashtoreth's mark can also be seen in those who pierce their bodies with "ornamental" jewelry. Participants have gone way beyond traditional pierced ears to puncture ear cartilage, tongues, lips, noses, eyebrows, navels, and privates. What's next? The American Red Cross disqualifies potential blood donors who have body piercing during its screening process because of the high risk of infections such as hepatitis, tetanus, tuberculosis and HIV associated with this practice.

There is a strong connection between homosexuality and the Ashtoreth spirit. In fact, homosexuality, lesbianism and cult prostitution were commonplace in the sexual rites associated with Ashtoreth ceremonial worship. Of course, that comes as no surprise because we know that idolatry itself leads to sexual degeneration and perverseness (Colossians 3:5). Could it be possible, then, that a strong homosexual community is the natural manifestation of the Ashtoreth (Jezebel) spirit?

Further study of the various Baal gods indicates that Ashtoreth had an extensive family of at least 70 other gods to which she gave birth. Baal, Dagon and Ashtoreth are but a few in a pantheon of gods referred to throughout history. These, however, are the most significant examples in our quest to identify the major characteristics of the Jezebel spirit. Our generation is a prime target for the greatest deception the world has ever seen.

JEZEBEL'S MESSENGER SPEAKS OUT

As you can imagine, I get all kinds of calls, letters and e-mails from fruits, flakes and nuts when I write about Jezebel and witchcraft. Here's an excerpt from a letter I received from one of Jezebel's messengers. I am including it to illustrate just how far along the road to deception people can travel hand in hand with the Jezebel spirit. A lost soul from New York writes:

"I would like to offer you another way of looking at history. After conducting months of research I discovered that Jezebel was born into a royal lineage. Her mother and father were the queen and king of Sidon. She was a Phoenician high priestess who was initiated into the sacred feminine mysteries of life, death and rebirth.

You are sadly mistaken about denigrating the feminine. You are projecting your own fear of your own femininity, and have tapped into the collective conscious and unconscious fear of women and her spiritual potential.

You are denying yourself a spiritual wisdom that nurtures, loves and regenerates. Read about archetypes. Queen Jezebel was murdered for worshipping the Mother, the ancient Mother of the Mediterranean. Jezebel ruled at a time in history where there was a political decline of the Mother goddess religion. The Christian fathers made everyone afraid of women, of her sacred body, of her ability to channel sacred spiritual energy from the Mother herself. You will never convince me otherwise.

Mark my words, the ancient Mother goddess is rising up out of the earth; the sacred serpent shall rise again. The sacred serpent is a symbol associated with the spiritual wisdom of life, death and rebirth, much like Christianity. Read your history and learn a new way of understanding the ancient Mother goddess. She is a deity. Hope to raise your consciousness.

In the next chapter, we will take a look at Jezebel's influence on the lukewarm Laodicean church.

SUMMARY
THE GODS OF JEZEBEL

Omri sealed his alliance with Phoenicia (current day Lebanon) through the marriage of his son Ahab to Jezebel.

The Sidonians worshipped two gods: Baal and Ashtoreth.

Whatever you prefer to call her, Ashtoreth and the spirit of Jezebel are one and the same. Jezebel manifests many traits of the Baal spirit.

Both Ahab and Jezebel were Ashtoreth and Baal worshipers.

King Ahab introduced idol worship into Israel by erecting a temple for Baal in Samaria where forbidden ceremonies were enacted (1 Kings 16:32).

Worship of the spirit of Baal separated the Israelites from Jehovah.

Baal is a god of prophetic divination.

Baal's title, "lord of the city," certainly reflects his serpentine assignment.

Ashtoreth is the "goddess of sex" and the "goddess of war."

There is a strong connection between homosexuality and the Ashtoreth spirit.

CHAPTER 4

JEZEBEL AND THE LAODICEAN CHURCH

Voice of Healing Prophet William Branham prophesied Jezebel's rise in 1933. Indeed, our generation is a prime target for the greatest deception the world has ever seen, and the Laodicean church will be the victim of that great deception.

In the Book of Revelation the Bible describes the condition of the Church right before the return of our Lord as lukewarm, which is neither cold nor hot. We learn that the Laodicean church is so distasteful to God that He spews it out of His mouth (Revelation 3:14-22). How did the Laodicean church become lukewarm? Through deception. Indeed, deceptions have already begun to sweep over local churches everywhere as leaders exchange the uncompromising, on-fire Gospel of Jesus Christ for watered-down, user-friendly messages. Are you a member of a Laodicean church? It is important to understand the pattern of this type of church because it is one in which Jezebel flows freely to deceive the sheep.

A GOSPEL THAT COSTS NOTHING?

What is the greatest deception in a Laodicean church? Probably presenting a bless-me-only Gospel that requires no change. How many people come into our churches and get "slain in the Spirit" at altar calls, only to come up off the carpet unchanged? Why is that happening? Perhaps because there is no repentance in the peoples' hearts. John the Baptist preached a Gospel that called for "fruits of repentance" (Matthew 3:8-10). But the Laodicean Gospel is one that carries no cross and no cost (Luke 14:27,33). You can get "saved" and never give up a thing. Just say a 30-second prayer, hand a membership card to your "seeker-friendly" pastor, and you're in. After all, as they say, "once saved, always saved."

A few years ago a dedicated member of our assembly with a sure call of God on his life left the church in a heated rage after I told him, "If you're in bed with any woman other than your wife when that trumpet sounds, then you won't enter the Kingdom of God" (Galatians 5:19-21). He didn't like that type of loving counsel because he was living in sin and unwilling to repent. Today that man is divorced and living with another woman out of wedlock. Sadly enough, a fly-by-night organization offering papers in the back of some "Christian" magazine recently ordained him as a minister. What kind of Gospel do you think he is preaching? This man's hidden transgression exposed him to the spirit of Jezebel, which thrives on lust and sexual sin.

FALSE SIGNS AND WONDERS

The Laodicean church has probably already produced more unstable and flaky Christians than any other time period in Christendom. That's at least partially because of the false signs and wonders that have deceived immature saints who are lukewarm and non-discerning. Every true move of God will produce mature, stable, relatable Christians, not spiritual fruits, flakes and nuts. The only way to bring about spiritual stability is through submission to God's Word and His leadership. While I realize all too well that there has been some abuse by supposed spiritual leaders in the

Body of Christ, there is still a righteous, godly leadership and we must submit ourselves to God's leaders. What spirit is it that would dislike true godly authority? Jezebel, of course. When the spirit of Jezebel enters into a local church that is full of deception, the fruit is usually persistent resistance to spiritual authority.

A primary peril for apostolic leadership is the Laodicean spiritual climate characterized by pride, control and merchandising. We must resist these temptations with everything in us and remain spiritually aware of the goings on in our local churches.

Today's Laodicean church is full of spiritual experiences, dreams, visions, New Age and personal prophecies. The Bible exhorts us to test the spirits (1 John 4:1), yet there is often a disdain by those with questionable motives to judge and examine these experiences. Have you ever felt the resistance from super spiritual people who take lightly the biblical instruction to "prove all things carefully and hold fast to that which is good" (1 Thessalonians 5:21)? One of the greatest dangers of the Laodicean movement will be false manifestations that produce only a soulish wonderment. I am not against supernatural encounters. I believe, emphatically, that there are true outpourings of the Spirit, but it is also wise to prove them because in doing so we are guarding ourselves from deception by Jezebel and other lying spirits.

FULL OF JEZEBEL'S DECEPTIONS

The spirit of Jezebel will be one of the greatest enemies of the Church in these last days, and she will use the Laodicean prophets, bearing smooth sayings through personal prophecy that includes hints of control and manipulation to further release a great deception into the land.

Remember that Jezebel had 450 prophets eating from her table. If the Prophetic Movement degenerates into nothing more than personal prophecies, this will play into, promote and strengthen the deception of Jezebel's divinations, further leading the Laodicean church into a false sense of security when all is certainly not well. Like sheep being led to the slaughter, this deception will be the fruit of seduction (Ezekiel 13:10).

It has been said that when God prophesies a "good word" to a person known to be living in sin that He is "calling those things that be not as though they were." That may be true. But it could very well be God answering that man according to the idolatry in his heart (Ezekiel 14:4). Lamentations 2:14 declares,

"Thy prophets have seen vain
and foolish things for thee:
and they have not discovered
thine iniquity, to turn away
thy captivity; but have seen
for thee false burdens and
causes of banishment"
(See also Isaiah 30:9-13).

I discuss this in detail in my book
Prophetic Operations.[1]

WILLIAM BRANHAM PROPHESIES JEZEBEL'S RISE

In 1933, William Branham, a well-known
"Voice of Healing" prophet, received seven
visions from the Lord. In the sixth vision
there arose, in the United States, a beautiful
woman clothed in splendor and royal robes.
This woman was given great power, and
she was beautiful, yet cruel, cunning and
deceitful. She dominated the land with her
authority. Brother Branham felt that she
represented an actual person or a particular
organization. I believe that this is a vision
of the rise of Jezebel in the last days. I
distinctively remember a great shift in the
Spirit over our nation in 1992 on the day
that Bill Clinton was sworn in as President
of the United States. Could this have marked

the beginning of the rise of this spirit? It is said that before Dr. Lester Sumrall went home to be with the Lord he commented that in the last days Jezebel would be the Church's greatest enemy. It is clear that Jezebel will use the her prophets with their smooth sayings and fortunetelling to further deceive the Laodicean church.

JEZEBEL'S PREDICTABLE PATTERN

Jezebel is sly but somewhat predictable. She operates in a pattern that I have seen countless times in local churches across the country. Are you discerning a Jezebel influence in your church? Here are six earmarks that will alert you to Jezebel's workings in your midst:

1. Jezebel targets leadership.

Listen, leader, Jezebel wants to get close to you — and fast. She looks to immediately infiltrate church leadership. Many times when God gives me a prophetic word that really punches the spiritual climate in our city it will stir these spirits to pay me a visit. They want to talk to me and me only. That throws up a big red flag with our ministry team.

2. Jezebel seeks
position in the local church.

There is nothing wrong with an eagerness to serve, but the spirit of Jezebel is looking for positions of authority, not positions of service. Much like the religious spirit, she wants to be in positions where she can be seen by men. She can't stand being in the shadow of others. She likes attention and places of control and will often begin inquiring about leadership opportunities as soon as she enters the church.

3. Jezebel creates soul ties.

Jezebel looks for hurt, wounded and discontent people. Why? Because she is a master at developing soul ties through the working of witchcraft. Read my book *Exposing Spiritual Witchcraft*[2] to get a better understanding of this demonic force and how it works.

4. Jezebel flows in personal prophecy.

Jezebel has prophetic words of personal prophecy for many. However, her prophetic utterances are typically crafted to feed spiritual pride. For example, she might deliver a word that sounds something like this, "The Spirit of God shows me that you are called to carry the Gospel into the nations of the earth. And I just sense that the people at this church really don't understand your unique calling like I do." Jezebel's prophetic motives are to separate you from those who can speak truth into your life. Remember, Jezebel seeks to draw people unto herself and she uses prophecy and flattery to fill the chairs at her dining room table. Flattery is a door into your heart. Beware of it and keep that door tightly shut up.

5. Jezebel starts private ministry.

When Jezebel delivers her false prophetic words she usually pulls people off to the side and away from others. I call this "private ministry" and it is a common practice of Jezebel. It doesn't take her long to create a super spiritual atmosphere in which to most effectively release her foul words. She is skillful at "hit and run" prophetic delivery. While many of her prophecies feed spiritual pride, Jezebel also tends to prophesy words that breed fear and suspicion. For example, she might say, "The Spirit of God shows me that something is wrong here, but I just can't get it all. Will you agree to pray with me until God shows me what's wrong with this church?" There is no need to receive prophecies that release fear. Prophetic gifting should edify (build you up spiritually in the

Lord), exhort (encourage you in the Lord) and comfort, according to 1 Corinthians 14:3. This is not to say that the Spirit of God does not speak of judgment; however, such serious prophetic words are usually reserved for those who refuse to repent and turn from their wicked ways.

6. Jezebel seeks information.

Jezebel is an information seeker. The Jezebel spirit thrives on information about what's happening around the church and in other's lives. Don't give her any! Knowledge of things that are none of her business only empowers this wicked spirit to manipulate and control in a more subversive manner. I could continue with lots of examples, but I think these are enough to make the point that we need to know our sheep, as well as those who labor among us (Proverbs 27:23; 1 Thessalonians 5:12).

Ask yourself the following questions to help determine if you are in a Laodicean church:

> Does the preaching tip toe around hard issues that would bring conviction to the hearers?

> Have you noticed a lot of rebellious attitudes and gossiping about leadership?

> Do you sense a red light in your spirit when you witness supposed outpourings of the Spirit or personal prophecies?
>
> Does the spiritual climate in your church seem dull, dead and devoid of the Spirit of God? Is it filled with tradition with little change? Is it "lukewarm"?

If you answered yes to any of these questions, then you may be sitting in the pews of a Laodicean church.

In the next chapter we begin to see how Jezebel uses messengers to release fear and change spiritual climates.

SUMMARY
JEZEBEL AND THE
LAODICEAN CHURCH

What is the greatest deception in a Laodicean church? Probably presenting a bless-me-only Gospel that requires no change.

When the spirit of Jezebel enters into a local church that is full of deception, the fruit is usually persistent resistance to spiritual authority.

The spirit of Jezebel will be one of the greatest enemies of the Church in these last days, and she will use the Laodicean prophets, bearing smooth sayings through personal prophecy that includes hints of control and manipulation to further release a great deception into the land.

Before Dr. Lester Sumrall went home to be with the Lord he commented that in the last days Jezebel would be the greatest enemy of the Church

There is nothing wrong with an eagerness to serve, but the spirit of Jezebel is looking for positions of authority, not positions of service.

Footnotes

1 Jonas Clark, Prophetic Operations (Hallandale, FL, Spirit of Life Publications, 2001)

2 Jonas Clark, Exposing Spiritual Witchcraft (Hallandale, FL, Spirit of Life Publications, 2003)

CHAPTER 5

JEZEBEL'S
SERIOUS THREATS

The Jezebel spirit is motivated by an insatiable hunger for power and control. The elements of conflict with Jezebel start with the threat and its messenger, and are shaped by our response. Let's face it, Jezebel's threats are serious. Will her menacing messages allow her to control your life or will you disregard her intimidating tactics?

Within the Laodicean church or out in the marketplace, Jezebel is a master at dispatching messengers of fear. Elijah met one of Jezebel's messengers shortly after a prophetic showdown with some false prophets on Mount Carmel. Elijah's fearful encounter demonstrates that the spirit of Jezebel is very active right before and right after a great victory. That's important to understand because just as Elijah had to contend with Jezebel's messengers during his ministry, so will you.

One of Jezebel's tactics is to use fear to either coerce you into making decisions that serve her ungodly purposes or stop you from going ahead with God's will for your life. Jezebel gets angry when you are making progress for God, and she will dispatch her eunuchs with terrorizing messages to draw you back to her table. The Jezebel spirit is motivated by an insatiable hunger for power and control. The elements of conflict with Jezebel start with the threat and its messenger, and are shaped by our response. Let's face it, Jezebel's threats are serious. Scripture chronicles Jezebel's frightening message to Elijah after he killed her false prophets:

> "Then Jezebel sent a messenger
> unto Elijah, saying, So let the
> gods do to me, and more also, if
> I make not thy life as the life of
> one of them by tomorrow about
> this time" (1 Kings 19:2).

In other words, "Elijah, I'm going to murder you for killing my prophets!" This was an evil forebode from a woman who had already proved her homicidal tendencies.

Has anyone ever told you that they were going to kill you, and you knew they had the power to carry out the deadly threat? I have, and more than once. The first time I received a death threat I was a young man. I was working the sales counter at a building material supply company when an armed robber came on the scene. As I approached the thief he stuck a gun right in my face and said, "Back off or I'm going to blow your brains out!" He could have killed me

The Jezebel spirit is motivated by an insatiable hunger for power and control.

instantly. But I did what he said and he left without incident. Praise God!

On a separate occasion another person threatened to shoot me after I caught him stealing power tools out of a warehouse. I could see the cold-blooded murder in his eyes. If you know someone has the ability to kill you, it makes you think differently. You will start praying in languages that you didn't even know you had.

When we read the Scripture's account of Jezebel's messenger, we need to understand that this was a serious threat. I can just see that messenger saying to Elijah, "Jezebel is going to kill you." Elijah knew she had the means and a heart evil enough back up her wicked words. After all, Jezebel's reputation preceded her as one known for killing the prophets of God.

JEZEBEL'S MESSAGE

The dangers of considering Jezebel's message are severe. Scripture records Elijah's response to this terrorist's words: "And when he saw (considered) that, he arose, and went for his life, and came to Beersheba, which belongeth to Judah, and left his servant there" (1 Kings 19:3). After his tremendous victory against the false prophets, Elijah suddenly lost his sense of spirituality. That's because when Elijah considered Jezebel's message, it birthed fear in him. And that fear convinced him to make a run for his life. It's one thing to run for safety so as to fight again, but Jezebel's message wounded Elijah. I don't want to be too hard on Elijah because I wasn't walking in his shoes, but he should not have considered what Jezebel's messenger had to say. He should have bound up those words, and sent the messenger back to Jezebel with a prophetic decree of his own, something like: "You're not going to kill me, but I'm coming after you!" Elijah should have reversed Jezebel's curse by reminding Jezebel that Jehovah is Lord.

The Jezebel spirit still sends demonic, even prophetic messages of fear to us today. Will we learn from Elijah's mistake? Or will we fall into the same trap, run to a far away place and ask God to put us out of our fear-laden misery? A false prophet once pronounced judgment on me because I wouldn't receive him as my personal prophet. He declared, "You're going to die in 30 days and your ministry is going to be as nothing." I was forced to deal very sternly with this man. When it comes to Jezebel's threats, we are not just talking about words written on a piece of paper that cause a sudden rush of adrenaline. No, we are talking about a spiritual force that releases a demonic assignment. This is the reason Elijah reacted as he did to Jezebel's message.

When the messenger released Jezebel's murderous words, a spirit of fear accompanied them. So when Elijah contemplated Jezebel's message, he opened himself up to the demonic assignments that were coupled with the communiqué. The end result was Jezebel's assignment hitting its target and fulfilling its purpose. When Elijah gave thought to the threat, it was like a demonic arrow hit his heart and released fear inside of him.

When the spirit of Jezebel attacks you, it will try and take you out of faith and drive you into fear. Even the memory of former victories in your life won't mean much to you. Instead, fear will hit you, and you'll feel like running away from your ministry, your calling, and God's anointing; you may even want to run from God Himself. Never bow to the spirit of fear. The Word says,

"For God hath not given us the spirit of fear; but of power, and of love, and of a sound mind" (2 Timothy 1:7).

I remember when the spirit of fear attacked my mind and tried to get me to consider its message. I took my family to Walt Disney World in Orlando, Florida on a Halloween night. There must have been 10,000 people there. My daughter Nichole was about three years old and she ran off into the crowd searching for one of the animated characters in the darkness of the night. It wasn't 10 seconds in between the time I turned around to grab a piece of candy for her and turned back around to hand it to her — and she was gone into the sea of people, many of whom were dressed up in demonic costumes. When I realized she was gone, a voice spoke into my imaginations saying, "I've got her and I'm going to keep her." All kinds of awful thoughts were bombarding my mind. These thoughts were messages from the spirit of fear. I had to be careful not to consider the message or to "tap into it" by agreeing with it. I had to say, "No, devil, I'm not going to receive that message from you. My daughter is alright and I will find her in a minute." I started praying in the Spirit and refused to entertain or speak fear's message. Within 30 minutes, Disney's security guards spotted her in an open theater watching some cartoons. She was safe and sound, laughing and playing. Praise the Lord! You, too, may have a messenger come to you prophesying fearful things. At that moment you have to discern, "Where did this message come from? Is this God's message or is this Jezebel's message?" If it's laced with fear, it's not from the Holy Spirit. It's extremely important that you lay hold of the right message.

Ask the following questions to help determine if you've considered Jezebel's message:

Have you ever felt like you lost a battle even though you know you won a tremendous victory?

Have you ever felt an unreasonable fear over something that you know is not likely to happen?

Have you ever felt compelled to dwell on a negative thought that someone introduced to you?

> Have you ever felt like you are taking two steps forward and one step back in your life?
>
> Have you ever felt like giving up because you had a bad day?

If you answered yes to any of these questions, then you may have considered Jezebel's message. Notice, too, the word "felt" in all of these questions. Jezebel loves to release her assignments in your emotions.

RESPONDING TO THE MESSAGE

How do we respond to the message of Jezebel? Unfortunately, many people tap into the message by believing and speaking it. Speaking Jezebel's message empowers it. Have you ever experienced that? You can pick up, prophesy and declare, Jezebel's plan in your house. I know that sounds a little strange, but it's true. You might say things like, "I'm giving up today. I just can't take it any more. I'm just going to quit." It's not God's will for you to talk like that. If you speak anything differently than God's will, then you are prophesying the wrong plan over your life. When you talk like that, you are verbalizing the wrong message. If your spouse gets into agreement with you and your defeatist confession, then you are really in trouble. Never forget that there is power in agreement both good and bad (Matthew 18:19). Every day we are going to get messages intended to take us out of God's will. If the messenger, Jezebel or anything else can get you into fear then it can rob your inheritance in Christ.

POTENTIAL MESSENGERS

Have you ever had somebody come into your home in a spiritual whirlwind, bursting through the door saying things like, "I have to talk to you right now. Get off the phone! You've got to hear this. Hurry! Hurry!" The next thing you know, this "crisis" conversation is beginning to stir you. It's amazing how easy it is to tap into the same spirit that someone brings into the room with them. You listen to their breaking news and, the next thing you know, you're leaving all in a huff on your way to meet a friend for lunch with that same spirit of strife on you. Then you pass it on to your lunch companion becoming a messenger of the unpleasant encounter you just experienced. Jezebel is always looking for potential messengers.

One day I had a staff meeting with our pastors and commented, "We have all types of people calling and visiting our church. Some call in despair, others call in anger. We, as staff, have to be careful that we don't tap into the same spirit that they are flowing in." In the church, on the home front or in the marketplace, we must not adopt the message or the spirit that Jezebel's messenger is carrying. We have to be very careful that we respond to people out of a right spirit and even more careful not to carry the message from a wrong spirit. I am still learning this principle of transference in ministry. I can be as right as right can be, but if I'm addressing an issue out of the wrong spirit, then I'm as wrong as the person that's wrong. So I have to be careful not to deal with people and issues out of the same spirit that they are flowing in just because they have stirred my spirit in some unseemly way. Can you see that? All of us have to be careful not to tap into and carry the wrong spirit. There are many examples of potential messengers. Have you ever seen somebody get into an argument, and the next thing you know they came at you with the same contentious spirit? They were so nice and wonderful before they left, then they came back distraught, depressed or angered. Many wives wonder what spirit their husband is going to come home with. Is he going to come home as he acts Sunday morning at church, or is he going to come home acting like the unsaved person he works with? Do you see what I mean? What spirit do we receive?

Let's not be a messenger of Jezebel — or any other spirit that is not of God.

Ask yourself the following questions to help determine if you are a potential messenger for Jezebel:

> When you get bad news, are you tempted to spread it around to others?
>
> Do you ever feel pulled to repeat a discouraging fact or opinion to those around you?
>
> Do you ever feel like responding to an angry person in anger?
>
> Do you feel that others are able to influence your emotions with their moods?
>
> Do you ever take negative moods home that were inspired by someone else?

If you answered yes to any of these questions, then you could be tapping into a wrong spirit.

Jezebel's messenger doesn't always work alone. Oftentimes her messenger has a companion who acts as a guard. Even though Scripture doesn't specifically expose this co-conspirator, sometimes experience can teach us a few things. This assistant is so common that it's important to point her out. I have experienced the onslaught of Jezebel's messengers and her various companions. These companions, or guards, accompany the messenger to strengthen and protect them as they go on their mission of destruction. Both Jezebel's messenger and its guard are eunuchs. Here's how this devilish duo works: First, the spirit of Jezebel will send you her prophetic message of fear and discouragement. Then look for the guard lurking about somewhere in the background. The enemy understands the spiritual dynamics of sending people out two by two. While the guard poses no direct threat, it often acts as a witness to gather information about your response to the message in order to feed Jezebel.

Ask yourself the following questions to help determine if one of Jezebel's messengers have paid you a visit:

> Have you ever received a phone call with an unreasonable complaint from a client who was threatening to stop doing business with you if you didn't agree to something that went against your moral standards?

Have you ever received an insane threat from someone who you are in competition with?

Have you ever talked with someone who delivered discouraging news, and then attempted to get you to wallow in it?

Have two people who seemed to oppose you with an ungodly common goal ever teamed up on you?

If you answered yes to any of these questions, then you may have met Jezebel's messenger — and its guard.

JEZEBEL RESPONDS

Jezebel doesn't always send messengers. Sometimes she confronts you herself. The following is an excerpt from a letter I received from a woman operating out of a Jezebel spirit. You don't even have to read between the lines to recognize this spirit fully manifested in the following words:

"You make me so proud to be the strong, independent, intelligent woman that I am. When I read misogynistic (women hating) writings such as yours, I know I've truly traveled the best of all paths. I once was a Sunday school teacher. Effeminate preachers railing against women who determined their own fate was part of the reason that I left Christianity to search for a better way. Thanks to men like you, I found it. I'm posting your web site on a few women's groups so they can point women in the right direction who haven't as yet made the decision to be strong and self-determinant. Anything that bleeds for seven days and does not die must be worshipped!"

In the next chapter we will look at the life of Ahab, who carries a provoking spirit as he uses Jezebel's seducing, warring abilities to advance his own selfish purposes.

SUMMARY
JEZEBEL'S SERIOUS THREATS

Jezebel is a master at dispatching messengers of fear.

The Jezebel spirit is motivated by an insatiable hunger for power and control.

Jezebel's reputation preceded her as one known for killing the prophets of God.

The dangers of considering Jezebel's message are severe.

When Elijah contemplated Jezebel's message, he opened himself up to the demonic assignments that were coupled with the communiqué.

Speaking Jezebel's message empowers it.

All of us have to be careful not to tap into and carry the wrong spirit.

Jezebel's messenger doesn't always work alone.

CHAPTER 6

AHAB THE PROVOKER

Ahab carries a provoking spirit. He is contentious, argumentative, depressive and hostile toward God's prophets. Ahab is not weak, but he does have insecurities that allow Jezebel to come in and usurp his authority. He will allow Jezebel to use her seducing, warring abilities to do his dirty work.

Throughout this book we have referenced the spirit of Jezebel. In this chapter we will take a look at her companion, King Ahab the provoker. Jezebel's husband Ahab is best known for his provoking spirit. Scripture says,

> "Ahab did more to provoke the LORD God of Israel to anger than all the kings of Israel that were before him" (1 Kings 16:33).

Can you imagine inflaming the Lord to such a degree that He would pen such a legacy for you? That makes it crystal clear how the Lord feels about the Ahab spirit. To provoke means to anger, irritate and annoy.

Those with the Ahab spirit have an annoying demeanor. They either go out of their way to say something offensive or simply abrade you with their actions. When you cross paths with the Ahab spirit, and we all have, you feel chided in your inner man. It's not always so much what they say. It can just as easily be the tone in which they say it or the spirit behind what they say that berates you. This spiritual clash with the Ahab spirit puts you in a defensive posture. That's because those who carry the Ahab spirit have an attitude problem. With various personalities, from bold and loud to weak and sneaky, Ahab is just plain annoying. He and his Queen Jezebel were a match made in hell.

AHAB THE CONTENTIOUS ONE

Scripture paints a picture of Ahab by comparing him to another notorious troublemaker. Scripture says that he walked in the sins of Jeroboam (1 Kings 16:31). This is very revealing because Jeroboam's name literally means "the contentious one." A contentious person is one who is quarrelsome. This contentious leader was known to ordain into ministry those who were not called by God (1 Kings 12:31-32). Just like Jeroboam, Ahab will surround himself with those of the lowest of character that are not divinely called into service. These are your classic "yes men" – and women. There are many with the Ahab spirit in ministry today who don't hesitate to ordain Jezebel (who is not called by God) or her eunuchs into ministry.

Ahab has a contentious, argumentative demeanor a kindred to Jeroboam. To contend means to strive, fight, compete, debate, dispute or stir up controversy. Ahab has a nit-picky persona that argues over the most trifling matters. This spirit is known to major in the minor and minor in the major and actively seeks out points of dispute during every day conversation. This overbearing, disagreeable attitude makes for a touchy spiritual climate wherever he goes. It's almost like someone saying, "I know what you are saying is true, but I'm going to challenge you just because that's my nature." That mind-set demonstrates Ahab's belligerent and pugnacious temperament.

AHAB THE STORM CARRIER

It's not just Jezebel that carries a whirlwind of calamity. Ahab brews up enough spiritual cyclones on his own. A man with an Ahab spirit once entered our office with such strife that it immediately morphed the spiritual climate in the entire building. It was so obvious that even those with little spiritual discernment couldn't help but take notice. You could literally feel the atmosphere tighten up as he made a colossal commotion over an innocent question. It was almost as if he brought a dark ominous cloud with him as he entered through the door. There may have been times when you have experienced

Ahab, reflecting one of the characteristics of the spirit of Baal, creates spiritual storms by making mountains out of molehills.

something similar. Perhaps you noticed your spirit conflict with someone in a room over something meaningless and you didn't know why. Could it have been a demonic spirit bent on stirring up trouble or picking a fight? Let's not forget that Ahab worshipped Baal, who was known as "the storm god." Since we gain understanding of people by studying the gods they serve, it's no surprise that one who worships "the storm god" would carry a storm with them wherever they go. Ahab, reflecting one of the characteristics of the spirit of Baal, creates spiritual storms by making mountains out of molehills.

Ask yourself the following questions to determine if you have met a modern-day Ahab:

> Do you know someone who insists on debating with you over even the most trivial matters?
>
> Have you met people that seem to go out of their way to be aggravating, annoying, irritating or provocative?
>
> Do you know anyone who always finds the fault in something and just has to point it out?
>
> Have you ever seen someone storm into the room in a whirlwind with a spirit of strife that changes the mood of the environment?

If you answered yes to any of these questions, then you have probably come face to face with Ahab.

AHAB'S COVETING DEPRESSION

To covet means to long with envy for what another person has. Ahab has a coveting spirit and falls into a state of deep depression if he doesn't get his way. Those with the Ahab spirit suffer with an ongoing struggle with depression. One day they're high on a cloud, and the next day they're in the depths of sorrow.

Jezebel's influence on Ahab intensifies his ungodly lust for the possessions of others. Just look at how Ahab behaved when Naboth wouldn't sell him his vineyard. Naboth was a small farmer that inherited some land near the king's palace. Scripture says after a failed negotiation to purchase his farm that,

> "Ahab came into his house heavy and displeased because of the word which Naboth the Jezreelite had spoken to him: for he had said, I will not give thee the inheritance of my fathers. And he laid him down upon his bed, and turned away his face, and would eat no bread" (1 Kings 21:4).

Ahab returned home frustrated and disappointed because he couldn't get his greedy hands on Naboth's vineyard. As Ahab laid down on his bed he sunk into such despair that he couldn't even eat. This illustrates Ahab's strong coveting spirit that drives him into a state of severe melancholy.

Like a vicious dog staring at a T-bone steak, Ahab salivated over Naboth's property — but to no avail. The Bible instructs us specifically about covetousness,

> "Neither shall thy desire thy neighbor's wife, neither shall thy covet thy neighbor's house, his field or his man servant or his maid servant, his ox, or his ass or anything that is thy neighbors" (Exodus 20:17).

Being rejected by Naboth threw Ahab into a state of depression. Ahab's dejection offers a grand opportunity for the Jezebel spirit to usurp one's rightful authority. More on Jezebel's hijacking of authority in a moment.

AHAB'S UPPITY ARROGANCE

The Bible is not the only place that records Ahab's tempestuous testimony. Josephus, a historian who lived from 37 A.D. to about 100 A.D. and was a member of the priestly aristocracy of the Jews, gives us some important insight into Ahab's dealings with Naboth. Josephus wrote, "Upon this the king was grieved as if he had received an injury" (notice how distressed Ahab was—when he could not get another man's possession.)

"It grieved him almost like he had been wounded some how, and he would neither wash himself nor take any food. And when Jezebel asked him what was troubling him he related to her the perverseness of Naboth and how his response was *beneath the royal authority*" (Italics added). Note King Ahab's uppity arrogance. His attitude was, "How dare Naboth, that mere peon, refuse me!" In his thinking, Naboth was an insignificant drudge who should realize his place as one bound in servitude to the king.

Ahab said that Naboth's response to him was "beneath the royal authority," thus revealing a deep pride in his heart. Ahab felt that Naboth had no right to talk to him like that, because, after all, he was the king. He felt slighted because Naboth wouldn't simply turn over his land. When Jezebel discovered Ahab strewn out on his bed in a deep depression, Jezebel was ready and waiting to make her move. Josephus wrote, "However (Jezebel) persuaded him not to be cast down at this accident but to leave off his grief and return to the usual care of his body for that she would take care to have Naboth punished." In other words, "Honey don't worry about it. I'll take care of Naboth for you." And so she did. The next text reveals that Jezebel immediately sent letters to the rulers of the Israelites in Ahab's name.

The spirit of Jezebel is an opportunist. She looks for any and every occasion to usurp your authority. Jezebel is watching and waiting for that moment when you are so distraught and depressed that you will hand her your authority on a proverbial silver platter. If you slip into a state of depression, be sure to guard yourself from the Jezebel spirit. Never give Jezebel your authority or let her represent you. Josephus continues,

The spirit of Jezebel is an opportunist.

"And (Jezebel) commanded them to fast and to assemble the congregation and to set Naboth at the head of them because he was of an illustrious family. She had three bold men, all ready to bear witness that Naboth had blasphemed God and the king. And then to stone him and to slay him in that manner. Accordingly when Naboth had been thus testified against as the queen had written to them, that he had blasphemed against God and Ahab the king, she desired him to take possession of Naboth's vineyard on free cost." Jezebel is a wicked spirit. Here we learn she will stop at nothing to reach her goals, even the murder of an innocent man. Jezebel set up Naboth with false accusations. What a wicked spirit! Then Jezebel had Naboth murdered and stole his property from him.

Jezebel is a murderer, and Ahab, by his inaction to stop her, is a murderer too.

Jezebel didn't care about Naboth's family or his right to preserve his inheritance and she doesn't care about yours, either. I wonder how many people have lost their family inheritance because Jezebel robbed them? I suspect it is pretty common, especially now in our perverse society where the abandonment of children is so prevalent.

There is another interesting note about Naboth: His name means "fruitful one." Jezebel cannot stand the fruit of the Spirit in a believer's life. Just as Jezebel destroyed the "fruitful one" she is also after the fruit of the Spirit of God in your life. She wants to rob you of joy, peace and love. As Josephus' chronicle illustrates, she will even set you up if that's what it takes — and Ahab will do nothing to stop her.

Josephus tells us another awful thing about Ahab: the news of a murder broke his depression. He writes, "Ahab was glad at what had been done and rose up immediately from the bed in where he laid to go and get Naboth's vineyard." Ahab's depression lifted immediately after Jezebel announced Naboth's death. The murder of an innocent man caused Ahab to shake off his woe-is-me attitude and rise up from his bed. Perhaps now you can see why God hates the evil spirit of Ahab so much.

AHAB IS NO WIMP

Because Ahab will let Jezebel do his fighting for him, we often tend to think that he is a wimp. I have known Ahab-type men, and I used to think they were just being abused by their Jezebel wives, and many times that is the case. Perhaps just as often, however, Ahab is showing his cunning in leveraging Jezebel's seducing, warring abilities to advance his own selfish purposes. Letting Jezebel do his dirty work leaves his hands looking clean. But make no mistake about it, God knows what's going on.

The mature Jezebel is attracted to men that are strong, rich and powerful. King Ahab was all three. Ahab didn't remain king by relaxing on his throne while Israel was fighting. No, the nation was constantly under attack and Ahab was a military commander. Military commanders are not weak. They are bold and militant. In fact, Ahab fought the Syrians who had an army of more than 100,000 men. When the Syrians began to attack Ahab, Josephus wrote that "he was grieved, yet he encouraged himself, and went to battle." So, again, Ahab-types are not necessarily weak, they are just emotionally insecure. Remember, those with the Ahab spirit have melancholy personalities that swing up and down like a manic yo-yo. It is only when Ahab has a down day that he allows Jezebel to supplant his authority. We can't let Ahabs off the hook by labeling them all as weak. Ahabs are as evil as Jezebel because they allow her to carry on without restraint.

AHAB AND SEXUAL SIN

We have already learned that Ahab was bound by fantasy because he served Baal, who, it was taught, was transported by fantasy. Those with the Ahab spirit have trouble with fantasy and perverse imaginations. They have a difficult time taking hold of their minds. They often have trouble sleeping at night because of mind traffic. Since the realm of fantasy and imaginations is also where pornography works, Ahabs are easily enticed by pornography and perverse inclinations. Sexual sin always seems to be intermingled in the Ahab and Jezebel relationship. That's because sexual sins and pornography are both part of the Ashtoreth spirit's influence. Pornography is a horrific thing that is destroying many lives. Those who view pornography open themselves up to the seductions of Ashtoreth (Jezebel), and all sorts of other demons.

AHAB IMPRISONS PROPHETS

Like Jezebel, Ahab loves the smooth words of false prophets. If he doesn't get one, however, he will seek retaliation against the one who delivered the unfavorable word. Look no further than the ministry of the Prophet Micaiah. When Ahab was building a confederacy with King Jehoshaphat, Jehoshaphat heard that Ahab had received prophecy from 400 prophets, all decreeing victory. Jehoshaphat was troubled by what he heard, and asked, "Do you have any of Jehovah's prophets around here?" Ahab responded reluctantly, "Yes, I have one, but he never says anything good about me, so I have him locked up. I won't let him out; he makes me mad every time I see him." (1 Kings 22:7-8).

Those who flow in the Ahab spirit thrive on prophecies that inflate their egos, serve their purposes and advance their egocentric causes. Micaiah wasn't like that. In fact, he told Ahab the way it was. Telling Ahab the truth, however, made him a target for attack and got him thrown in prison.

AHAB THE MERCHANDISER

Scripture also makes it clear that Ahab will follow the merchandising ways of Baalim. When Elijah confronted Ahab, God declared that he had followed the way of Baalim,

> "And (Elijah) answered, I have not troubled Israel; but thou,

and thy father's house, in that ye have forsaken the commandments of the LORD, and thou hast followed Baalim" (1 Kings 18:18).

Baalim was the prophet of God that Balak, the king of Moab, enticed to curse the children of Israel with a bribe. To Balaam's surprise, he could not fulfill his obligation to curse Israel because they had been blessed by God. Balaam, once God's prophetic voice, was overcome by his own lust for riches, honor and promotion. Since Balaam was not able to curse the children of Israel, he told the king of Moab to send seducing women into Israel's camp (Numbers 25). This instruction, Balaam's greatest sin, would cause the children of Israel to break covenant with Jehovah. Balaam is known as the prophet who sold his prophetic gift from God. In fact, he is the one most thought of as a merchandiser of the gifts of God. Ahab, like Balaam, followed in the same merchandising sins of Balaam, seeking riches, honor and promotion.

AHAB'S ABANDONMENT

Ahab will abandon his loved ones to keep from contending with Jezebel. The Jezebel spirit likes to keep Ahab stirred up.

To stir up means to stimulate, entice, move, persuade or provoke. Scripture says,

> "But there was none like unto Ahab, which did sell himself to work wickedness in the sight of the LORD, *whom Jezebel his wife stirred up*" (1 Kings 21:25 Italics added).

Listen to the stories of children whose fathers divorced their mothers in order to remarry a woman with a Jezebel spirit. Oftentimes you will discover that these children lost their family inheritance due to Jezebel's thieving pilferage. Children will very often tell you that their father didn't want to battle with Jezebel because he did not feel he could match her ruthlessness. So instead the father bowed out from the battle, choosing to walk away from his family. That's one demonstration of the Ahab spirit at work in the family.

Jezebel will stir Ahab into a disgusting complacency. One man told me that he "caught hell" from Jezebel after his grown children from his first marriage came over to visit. Instead of putting his new wife in her place, he would avoid and distance himself from his children just to steer clear of the aftermath of Jezebel. That's another manifestation of the Ahab spirit on the home front. Her intimidation persuaded him to compromise his willingness to resist her. The spirit of Jezebel will wear Ahab down through continued badgering for the purpose of usurping his authority as head of the house. Don't feel sorry for Ahab because he thinks it's worth it. He tolerates Jezebel because he uses her to fight his personal wars for him. In a sense, Ahab creates his own monster because he is full of insecurities and will draw on Jezebel's warring strength to fill that place of weakness.

In the next chapter we will find inspiration in Jehu — Jezebel's nemesis. We can learn how to deal with this controlling spirit from a true apostle of war.

SUMMARY
AHAB THE PROVOKER

Ahab carries a provoking spirit.

Ahab uses the seducing and warring abilities of Jezebel to advance his own selfish purposes.

Ahab is contentious and argumentative.

Ahab makes mountains out of molehills.

Ahab suffers from severe cases of depression.

Ahab struggles with fantasy and imaginations.

Ahab is enticed by riches, honor and promotion.

Ahab will abandon his own children rather than contend with Jezebel.

Ahab is full of fear and will draw on Jezebel's warring strength to fill that place of weakness.

CHAPTER 7

JEZEBEL'S NEMEMIS

God called and empowered Jehu, an apostle of war,
to conquer Jezebel, a goddess of war, and to destroy
the house of Ahab.

All believers have spiritual assignments working against them that they do not always recognize, understand or have the ability to explain. When we read books like this, it exposes those unseen assignments and enables us to better comprehend what we are feeling and sensing.

You have learned some powerful truths about Jezebel in the previous chapters. You know how to identify her and are aware of the ways in which she attacks. Now let's read about her nemesis — Jehu. We can glean volumes about destroying the ill affects of the Ahab and Jezebel spirits by studying the life and ways of Jehu.

JEHU THE COMMANDER

Scripture testifies of a man called Jehu whom God raised up in the days of King Ahab and Jezebel. God anointed him as an apostle of war, and commissioned him to battle our two evil rulers and travel throughout the land uprooting their evil affects. Jehu was a very interesting combatant and serves as our biblical example of what it takes to overcome the spirit of Jezebel.

We first learn of Jehu when Elisha sends a messenger to him. This herald refers to him as captain,

> "And when (Elisha's messenger) came, behold, the captains of the host were sitting; and he said, I have an errand to thee, O captain. And Jehu said, Unto which of all us? And he said, To thee, O captain" (2 Kings 9:5).

This is very revealing because the word "captain" means commander. A commander is not merely a passive believer in Jehovah. The term commander is indicative of one with spiritual ranking, strength and fortitude, all traits necessary to successfully contend with Jezebel.

In this passage, God sent His prophet to anoint Jehu with a powerful warring grace. Let's take a look at Jehu's calling.

> "And he arose, and went into the house; and he poured the oil on (Jehu's) head, and said unto him, Thus saith the LORD God of Israel, I have anointed thee king over the people of the LORD, even over Israel. And thou shalt smite the house of Ahab thy master, that I may avenge the blood of my servants the prophets, and the blood of all the servants of the LORD, at the hand of Jezebel" (2 Kings 9:6-7).

So we see that not only did the Lord call him into kingship but He also commissioned him to avenge the deaths of His servants.

Remember, Jezebel was known for murdering the prophets of God. Because Ahab continued to serve the Baal and Ashtoreth gods, Jehovah sent Elijah his way, saying, "Go tell Ahab it will not rain on this land except at My word." In obedience to Jehovah, Elijah delivered the prophetic announcement and we know that it did not rain for three and a half years. The result of this prophetic announcement was a severe famine in the land. Josephus, our historian, documented a famine that was not just local, but throughout the entire world.

Why the famine? God was getting everyone's attention. Unfortunately, Jezebel was so angry with Elijah's decree that she killed every prophet of Jehovah that she could find. However, God saw her evil design and found Himself an apostle of war to battle a goddess of war. Let's continue to read the prophetic call on Jehu's life. Scripture says,

> "For the whole house of Ahab shall perish: and I will cut off from Ahab him that pisseth against the wall, and him that is shut up and left in Israel: And I will make the house of Ahab like the house of Jeroboam the son of Nebat, and like the house of Baasha the son of Ahijah: And the dogs shall eat Jezebel in the portion of Jezreel, and there shall be none to bury her. And he opened the door, and fled" (2 Kings 9:8-10).

LAND OF REVELATION

This prophetic decree represents the scope of Jehu's mandate. From it we learn the future of Ahab and Jezebel. Before we read how Jehu defeated them, however, it's important to understand the spiritual significance of where they lived. These royal rioters lived in a place called Jezreel in the land of Samaria. That land was given to one of the 12 tribes of Israel called Issachar. Issachar was the tribe known to flow in revelation, and who,

> "understood the times and the seasons of God and what Israel ought to do" (1 Chronicles 12:32).

Jezreel is the place Ahab built a temple for Baal and Ashtoreth; the very place called "revelation." Can you see the parallel? The Jezebel spirit set up her throne in the land of revelation. It is spiritual revelation that is vital in our lives. Without it we can never deeply know our Lord.

THE SEVEN BATTLES OF JEHU

Jehu received a specific commission from God:

> "smite the house of Ahab" (2 Kings 9:7).

To smite is the Hebrew word *nakah*, meaning to attack, punish, kill, chastise, conquer, subjugate, ravage, beat, scourge, capture or slay. Jehu had the Spirit of power and might upon him. He was a commander possessing spiritual ranking, strength and fortitude who carried authority and a divine commission.

While Jehu's mandate was to smite the house of Ahab, it required seven separate battles to accomplish that heavenly goal. By examining each of these battles we can learn the scope of our warfare and our ultimate victory. Our warrior Jehu defeated:

> Joram, who exalts himself against God.

> Ahaziah, who steals our possessions.

> Jezebel, who buffets our revelation.

> Ahab's 70 grandsons, all controllers born in the house of control.

> The brethren of Ahaziah, eunuchs who honor Ahab and Jezebel.

Ahab, the provoking contentious one.

Divination and false government.

THE FIRST BATTLE: JEHU VS. JORAM (THE EXALTED ONE)

Jehu fought several different battles. The first one was against a man named Joram. Joram's name means "exalted one." He was Jezebel's son. Let's read the testimony of this engagement.

> "And it came to pass, when Joram saw Jehu, that he said, Is it peace, Jehu? And he answered, What peace, so long as the whoredoms of thy mother Jezebel and her witchcrafts are so many? And Joram turned his hands, and fled, and said to Ahaziah, There is treachery, O Ahaziah. And Jehu drew a bow with *his full strength*, and smote Joram between his arms, and the arrow went out at his heart, and he sunk down in his chariot" (2 Kings 9:22-24 Italics added).

Facing an eminent threat from Jehu, Joram wanted to make peace. Jehu, however, would not take his focus off of his divine mission. He made it very clear that Jezebel's whoredoms and witchcrafts had to be rooted out. When Joram saw the uncompromising militancy of Jehu, he fled for his life.

> "Then said Jehu to Bidkar his captain, Take up, and cast him in the portion of the field of Naboth the Jezreelite: for remember how that, when I and thou rode together after Ahab his father, the LORD laid this burden upon him; Surely I have seen yesterday the blood of Naboth, and the blood of his sons, saith the LORD; and I will requite thee in this place, saith the LORD. Now therefore take and cast him into the plat of ground, according to the word of the LORD" (2 Kings 9:25-26).

The Bible tells us that Jehu, with "full strength" pulled back an arrow and shot Joram, the "exalted one" right in the back and through the heart (2 Kings 9:24). Notice that Jehu was operating in "full strength" when battling Jezebel's son. Spiritual strength is developed in us by being a doer of the Word and facing every spiritual challenge that comes our way. Jehu teaches us a valuable lesson as he refuses to compromise his call by making peace with Joram. He quickly took him out.

THE SECOND BATTLE:
JEHU VS. AHAZIAH
(THE ONE THAT STEALS POSSESSIONS)

Ahaziah was another one of Jezebel's sons. Ahaziah represents Jezebel's thieving spiritual sons and daughters that steal our inheritance.

> "But when Ahaziah the king of Judah saw this, he fled by the way of the garden house. And Jehu followed after him, and said, Smite him also in the chariot. And they did so at the going up to Gur, which is by Ibleam. And he fled to Megiddo, and died there. And his servants carried him in a chariot to Jerusalem, and buried him in his sepulcher with his fathers in the city of David" (2 Kings 9:27-28).

So we learn that Jehu returned from conquering Joram only to face another battle against another of Jezebel's evil spawn. Ahaziah's name means the "one that has taken possessions." Ahaziah was an evil man, according to the Scriptures.

> "Ahaziah the son of Ahab began to reign over Israel in Samaria the seventeenth year of Jehoshaphat king of Judah, and reigned two years over Israel. And he did evil in the sight of the LORD, and walked in the way of his father, and in the way of his mother, and in the way of Jeroboam the son of Nebat, who made Israel to sin: For he served Baal, and worshipped him, and provoked to anger the LORD God of Israel, according to all that his father had done" (1 Kings 22:51-53).

Jehu went after the thief Ahaziah with a passion. One of the most common traits of the Jezebel clan is its members' ability to steal what rightfully belongs to you. Have you lost any possessions to their brood? The Jehu anointing will stop those thieves every time.

After Jehu slew two of Jezebel's children, he turned toward Jezreel where he targeted none other than the wicked Queen Jezebel herself.

THE THIRD BATTLE:
JEHU VS. JEZEBEL
(THE ONE WHO OCCUPIES
THE LAND OF REVELATION)

One of the most important aspects of Jehu's anointing is its ability to open a way for prophetic revelation. When we understand Jezebel's ability to hinder the voice of the prophets through occupying the land of Jezreel we discover how important Jehu's calling really was. Let's take a look.

"And when Jehu was come to Jezreel, Jezebel heard of it; and she painted her face, and tired her head, and looked out at a window. And as Jehu entered in at the gate, she said, Had Zimri peace, who slew his master? And he lifted up his face to the window, and said, Who is on my side? who? And there looked out to him two or three eunuchs. And he said, Throw her down. So they threw her down: and some of her blood was sprinkled on the wall, and on the horses: and he trode her under foot" (2 Kings 9:30-33).

Jezebel stepped to the edge of her tower, looked out of her window with painted face and called Jehu "Zimri." Zimri was a ruler that assassinated a king and later committed suicide. This statement is one last ditch effort to deter Jehu by releasing witchcraft against him. Jezebel is really prophesying, "If you kill me then you will commit suicide just like Zimri did." Jehu, however, would not be moved by this false prophecy. Unlike Elijah, who considered Jezebel's message, Jehu was bold and aggressive in the face of her serious threats. Jehu squared off with Jezebel and commanded her own eunuchs to throw her down. Jezebel died in the streets, thus fulfilling the prophetic word of Elijah the Tishbite.

> "And when (Jehu) was come in, he did eat and drink, and said, Go, see now this cursed woman, and bury her: for she is a king's daughter. And they went to bury her: but they found no more of her than the skull, and the feet, and the palms of her hands. Wherefore they came again, and told him. And he said, This is the word of the LORD, which he spake by his servant Elijah the Tishbite, saying, In the portion of Jezreel shall dogs eat the flesh of Jezebel: And the carcass of Jezebel shall be

as dung upon the face of the field in the portion of Jezreel; so that they shall not say, This is Jezebel" (2 Kings 9:34-37).

Thus we learn of the ultimate fate of Jezebel: to be eaten by dogs.

THE FOURTH BATTLE: JEHU VS. 70 GRANDSONS OF AHAB (CONTROLLERS BORN IN THE HOUSE OF CONTROL)

After Jezebel's death, Jehu pursued the 70 sons of Ahab. He went after them with a great zeal and did not stop until he had fulfilled his mission.

"And Ahab had seventy sons in Samaria. And Jehu wrote letters, and sent to Samaria, unto the rulers of Jezreel, to the elders, and to them that brought up Ahab's children, saying, Now as soon as this letter cometh to you, seeing your master's sons are with you, and there are with you chariots and horses, a fenced city also, and armour; Look even out the best and meetest of your master's sons, and set

him on his father's throne, and
fight for your master's house"
(2 Kings 10:1-3).

As Jehu pursued the 70 sons of Ahab he
sent a demand letter to their guardians in
the town. He said, "Since you are harboring
the grandsons of Ahab, choose one of them
and make him a king. Then get your warriors
together, come out, and let's fight." They sent
a letter back to Jehu and said, "No way!"
Jehu then wrote a second letter saying,

> "If ye be mine, and if ye will
> hearken unto my voice, take
> ye the heads of the men your
> master's sons, and come to me
> to Jezreel by to morrow this
> time. Now the king's sons, being
> seventy persons, were with the
> great men of the city, which
> brought them up. And it came
> to pass, when the letter came to
> them, that they took the king's
> sons, and slew seventy persons,
> and put their heads in baskets,
> and sent him them to Jezreel"
> (2 Kings 10:6-7).

Responding to Jehu's demands, the
caretakers of Ahab's sons went into their
rooms with a sword, cut off their heads,

put them in baskets and delivered them
to Jehu. That's ruthless, but it spared the
entire city from the wrath of God. Jezebel,
too, is a ruthless militant, and when God
decides to execute judgment on her it won't
be a pretty sight.

Old Testament battles are natural
examples of spiritual truths. God sent Jehu,
the apostolic warrior, to smite and utterly
destroy the whole house of Ahab, including
his children. Scripture says,

> "So Jehu slew all that remained
> of the house of Ahab in Jezreel,
> and all his great men, and his
> kinsfolks, and his priests, until
> he left him none remaining"
> (2 Kings 10:11).

THE FIFTH BATTLE:
JEHU VS. THE BRETHREN OF AHAZIAH
(THE EUNUCHS OF JEZEBEL)

Those eunuchs who honor Jezebel will
not escape the notice of the Lord. They were
next on God's agenda. Scripture says,

> "Jehu met with the brethren
> of Ahaziah king of Judah, and
> said, Who are ye? And they
> answered, We are the brethren
> of Ahaziah; and we go down to

salute the children of the king and the children of the queen. And he said, Take them alive. And they took them alive, and slew them at the pit of the shearing house, even two and forty men; neither left he any of them" (2 Kings 10:13-14).

After this Jehu went to Samaria, and 42 men greeted him on his way. Jehu asked, "Where are you men going?" They responded, "We're going to talk to the queen mother." Jehu replied, "Really?" "Yes," they said, "we are relatives and we wanted to come down and greet everybody and make sure that the royal family is doing well." Jehu responded, "What a coincidence, I just left there." (I'm paraphrasing, of course.)

Next, Jehu commanded his men to take these supporters of Ahab and Jezebel and execute them.

These men (possibly either more sons or simply friends of the family) were in the wrong place at the wrong time meeting the wrong guy. That's how consumed Jehu was with carrying out his ministry. He had a divine tenacity about him. He was on a mission from God, and he knew exactly what he was called to do. He let no one escape. All of this teaches us the uncompromising zeal that Jehu demonstrated in fulfilling God's call on his life.

THE SIXTH BATTLE:
JEHU VS. THE HOUSE OF AHAB
(PROVOKING CONTENTIOUS ONES)

Finally, Ahab, the king who did more to provoke the Lord to anger than any king before him, met his fate at Jehu's hand. Scripture declares,

> "And Jehu said, Come with me, and see my zeal for the LORD. So they made him ride in his chariot. And when he came to Samaria, he slew all that remained unto Ahab in Samaria, till he had destroyed him, according to the saying of the LORD, which he spake to Elijah" (2 Kings 10:16-17).

Now Jehu was ready to finish the job. He went into Samaria and sought out the rest of Ahab's house who were living or hiding throughout the territory. All that he found, he slew.

THE LAST BATTLE:
JEHU VS. BAAL WORSHIPPERS
(DIVINATION AND FALSE GOVERNMENT)

Jehu's last act of war was to enter one of the cities in which there was a temple built to Baal. We can only assume that this was a main edifice Ahab built to worship a foreign god. Jehu, with camouflaged intent, declared a day of worship to Baal saying, "Everybody in this city that worships Baal, come and let's have a feast and a grand sacrifice." About 3,000 people came to the temple of Baal, where Jehu had all his mighty men of war dress the Baal worshipers with identifying vestments. Of course, Baal worship was strictly forbidden by Jehovah. It represented the demonic forces of divination and false government and it had to be dealt with. So Jehu entered the temple to watch the Baal worshipers and the prophets of Baal offer sacrifices during their worship service. That's when Jehu, ready to complete his purpose, commanded his officers to look around them and to make sure that there were none of Jehovah's servants at the meeting. When all was clear, Jehu ordered his men to surround the temple and kill all who were dressed in the apparel of the Baal worshipers.

With that sweeping act, Jehu, Jezebel's nemesis, concluded his assignment: to "go and smite the house of Ahab."

We, too, have an assignment to smite the house of Ahab with a Jehu anointing that won't compromise with Jezebel's seducing tactics.

In the next chapter we will learn more about the full-strength anointing with which God empowered Jehu to invade and conquer Jezebel's treachery.

SUMMARY
JEZEBEL'S NEMESIS

Jehu was an "apostle of war."

Jehu is our example of what it takes to defeat the spirit of Jezebel.

A commander is indicative of one with spiritual ranking, strength and fortitude, all traits necessary to successfully contend with Jezebel.

God sent His prophet to anoint Jehu with a powerful warring grace.

Ahaziah represents the thieving spiritual sons and daughters of Jezebel that steal our inheritance.

The offspring of Ahab and Jezebel are thieves.

Unlike Elijah, who considered Jezebel's message, Jehu was bold and aggressive against her.

Jehu squared off with Jezebel and commanded her own eunuchs to throw her down.

Jezebel died in the streets, thus fulfilling the prophetic word of Elijah the Tishbite.

Old Testament battles are natural examples of spiritual truths.

Those eunuchs who honor Jezebel will not escape the notice of the Lord.

CHAPTER 8

SHIGGAOWN TENACITY

It takes ruthless faith and militant determination to defeat the Jezebel spirit. Jezebel is not all-powerful. She can be conquered, and God desires to spiritually equip you to be the one to do it.

Jehu's chariot symbolized his aggressiveness. As Jehu pursued Jezebel's son Joram, who was hiding in Jezreel, Scripture says he was driving his chariot furiously (2 Kings 9:20). This is a fascinating description of Jehu, who could be recognized from afar by his mastery of a chariot. The word furiously (from the Hebrew word *shiggaown*) signifies that Jehu had a militant determination and fierceness about him. The quintessence of the word shiggaown likens the one it describes to an insane man. This word choice reveals Jehu's unyielding focus and resolve. Jehu did not let anything stand in his way or propel him from his purpose. We, too, should have the same fervent grit that characterizes Jehu.

All of us are called to overcome the spirit of Jezebel. Scripture says,

> "For whatsoever is born of God overcometh the world: and this is the victory that overcometh the world, even our faith" (1 John 5:4).

The word overcome (from the Greek word *nikao*) is an interesting word, meaning "to carry off the victory." Jehu proved his faith as a victorious conqueror. His natural victories were indications of spiritual victories. Jehu didn't just battle Ahab and Jezebel when they happened to cross his path, he aggressively went after them. He hunted them down, and even destroyed their high places of worship. In doing so, Jehu demonstrated a ruthless faith in God and carried off the victory.

Some say they want to go to an average church. But average people in average churches do not demonstrate ruthless faith. Like average people, mediocre churches will not get the job done. Don't be average. The average church has a reputation of being a lifeless church, a lukewarm church, a Laodicean church. Average is the enemy of best. It takes ruthless faith and militant determination to defeat the Jezebel spirit.

Trust God, do His Word, get planted in the right church and see yourself as a victorious believer who has overcome all obstacles.

JEZEBEL'S WHOREDOMS

The Bible says that Jehu hated Jezebel's whoredoms — her sexual sins (2 Kings 9:22).

The Ashtoreth spirit leads people into fornication, adultery, homosexuality, prostitution and sexual perversion of all sorts. The Catholic church has been overwhelmed with priests convicted of homosexual child molestation. Could it be the direct result of Ashtoreth's ability to create eunuchs through sexual whoredoms? If you are having problems with sexual imaginations or seducing fantasies you could be under the attack of Jezebel. Seducing fantasies, imaginations, homosexuality and pornography are all manifestations of Jezebel's whoredoms. After all, she is the "seducing goddess of war."

JEHU'S BOW

In the last chapter we learned that Jehu drew his bow with full strength when attacking Joram (2 Kings 9:24). Jehu refused to hold back. He was fully committed to his cause and the Word of God. If we are going to defeat the spirit of Jezebel we, like, Jehu, must be fully committed to serving our Lord Jesus Christ. One cannot triumph over Jezebel without being obedient to the Word of God. It's vital to be a doer of the Word and not merely a hearer who deceives his own self (James 1:23). An apathetic attitude toward the Word of God endangers believers with deception, the area where Ashtoreth dwells.

It takes ruthless faith and militant determination to defeat the Jezebel spirit.

Perhaps the greatest spiritual opposition one encounters is against fervent effectual prayer. Where Jezebel reigns, hard heavens abound. A hard heaven is an area where it seems as though your prayers are reaching the ceiling of your house only to bounce back to the ground. A hard heaven is an atmosphere in which you are doing everything the Word tells you to do, but nothing seems to be working. A hard heaven is what often causes people to skip church services, cut back on praying, worshipping God, giving financial offerings to advance the Gospel, or doing just about anything other than spiritual things. Many Christians report difficulty praying when the heavens are hard. I am convinced that the spiritual resistance one feels during times of prayer is a signal of spiritual warfare. If you discipline yourself to press in and pray anyway, then after a while it won't be hard to overcome any spiritual opposition you might face. Never back away from spiritual resistance because we are assured the Greater One lives inside of us. Every believer should make it a priority to order his or her prayer life and learn how to fight back through intercession.

Warfare prayer is an important revelation to our generation. When I was a young man we didn't have the revelation that we could fight back through intercession. Life was simply a matter of trusting in God's sovereignty. We didn't know that prayer changes things. Some people had a defeatist attitude and would sing songs with verses like, "One more day, one more heavy load, one more burden and we will all be there soon." Today, however, we've learned a thing or two about prayer. We recognize that through God's power, might, strength, Word, and our heartfelt prayers, He changes things. In fact, through prayer, God changes everything. That's good news! Yes, we can take heart in knowing that prayer causes our circumstances to line up with God's Word regardless of what's going on around us.

When we started Spirit of Life Ministries in Hallandale Beach, Fla., a territorial spirit took on the assignment of intimidating us. That spirit said things like, "Don't sing too loud. Don't teach like that. You're too radical. You're too wild. No one will attend the services if you pray like that," and so on, and so on, and so on. All of those spiritual accusations were a release by dark forces attempting to terrorize us in order to get us out of God's will. It felt awful when we prayed, but we were compelled to press through our feelings until we got the victory. Thank God He gave us the grace to press in and press on.

God also gave Jehu the grace to press. Jehu was a man of indomitability who was relentless in his pursuit of Jezebel. To pursue means to follow, to overtake, strive to obtain or accomplish, annoy and trouble.

Some believers still don't have the pursuing faith that's vital to overthrowing the Jezebel spirit. They want everybody else to do their praying, fighting and believing for them. They are not willing to make any effort of their own. These are immature Christians and Jezebel will eat them for lunch the first chance she gets so that they never can blossom and grow in Christ. The Church is awaking, however, to Her spiritual authority to oppose powers that oppress regions, territories and cities. Yes, the Body of Christ is beginning to pursue its divine rights as sons and daughters of faith. The Apostle Paul is a good example of one who exercised his authority, opposed the working of a goddess, and pursued his heavenly call.

Ephesus was the city where Paul built his flagship church. It was the place where he demonstrated an apostolic grace and taught the Body of Christ how to live successfully. Diana of Ephesus was a fertility goddess with the same attributes as Ashtoreth and was the beast that Apostle Paul wrestled at Ephesus (Acts 19). Paul's victory over the goddess put a damper on the local idol selling business. The city's merchants started an uproar because they blamed Paul for costing them money. How did Paul defeat this type of Jezebel? When he entered Ephesus, he entered with a fervent spirit to invade that city with the Gospel of Jesus Christ. It never entered his heart to compromise his purpose by ignoring the idolatry of Diana worship. Paul, like Jehu, had shiggaown tenacity. He teaches us that the Gospel of Jesus Christ is a war cry against demonic principalities and powers and that we are all called to overcome their rule. Scripture confirms this declaring,

> "From the days of John the
> Baptist until now the kingdom
> of heaven suffers violence and

the violent take it by force"
(Matthew 11:12).

Overcoming the Jezebel spirit requires a level of spiritual intercession that is violent in faith toward the things of God. To be spiritually violent in faith means to have an intense force, be ardent and balanced, yet extreme, and act with a strong, uncompromising spirit.

THE MEANING OF JEHU'S NAME

We have discussed many Bible characters throughout this book, including Ahab, Jezebel, Elijah and Jehu. Jehu, moreover, is our hallmark to learning how to defeat the Jezebel spirit. It wasn't Elijah the prophet who took Jezebel out, rather God's warrior Jehu. The acts of this apostle of war serve as our blueprint for defeating both Ahab and Jezebel.

Let's dissect the various meanings of Jehu's name.

Jehu translates "Jehovah Is."

Jehu was the son of Jehoshaphat, whose name means, "Jehovah Judges."

> Jehu was also the grandson of Nimshi, which means, "one who sets free."

> When combined, Jehu's heritage translates like this — "Jehovah Is He Who Judges and Sets Free."

So, when the Jehu spirit is in operation, Jehovah God, the one Who Is, judges wickedness and sets captives free. That is exactly what Jehu did when he destroyed Ahab's house. Jehu judged and set the people free.

Scripture says that Jehu was anointed for battle. He was also a person that demonstrated spiritual power and might. Remember, Jehu was divinely commissioned to smite the whole house of Ahab.

We, too, are called to flow in the same spirit of power and might that Jehu carried (Ephesians 6:10). When we square off with Jezebel we must not depend on our own fleshly strength, but on the wisdom and anointing of the Holy Spirit. God raised up Jehu, an apostle of war, to defeat a goddess of war. Do you see that? He did it in order to break the powers of the Ashtoreth and Baal spirits that were deceiving or murdering God's prophets and turning others toward idolatry. God used Jehu to make a way for righteousness in the land.

A BOLD PURSUIT

It's important to note that the servant of Elisha came to the "Commander" Jehu, a man of spiritual ranking. That's because Elisha knew that those who are able to successfully contend with Jezebel must have a measure of spiritual fortitude. Of course, those with spiritual ranking are not casual church-going Christians. Nor do they float from church to church, never really plugging in anywhere. Spiritual fortitude, once again, comes from being a doer of the Word. That means not forsaking the gathering of ourselves together in the local church where there is a corporate anointing and a spiritual impartation through the laying on of hands that offers strength for the battle. And spiritual ranking only comes out of a dedicated relationship with Jesus and the Holy Spirit.

Just like Jehu, modern-day Christian commanders have a take-charge propensity. Jehu wasted no time in pursuing the house of Ahab after he received his commission. I have seen people receive a divine mandate from heaven only to continue to sit around and do nothing. They talk the anointing right off themselves and start wondering if they were really called in the first place. Stay away from talk ministry. When God calls you to do something don't sit around in apathy, be like Jehu and go for it!

Jehu understood his command to smite his enemies. Do we truly understand ours? Such Jehu-like aggressiveness appears to be somewhat of a mystery in our generation. Jehu understood his calling and laid hold of it. He didn't concern himself with what the other captains around town were doing. He was consumed with fulfilling his own call. He had an apostolic appointment with the house of Ahab, and rushed to get there on time. How many people hear what the Spirit of God is saying to them, yet never really grab hold? How many never leave their comfort zones and pursue their destinies? To be like Jehu we must lay hold of our divine purpose. Jehu immediately jumped into battle. This is the shiggaown tenacity that we must also exhibit to conquer Jezebel.

STRONG FLESH AND WEAK SPIRITS

Back to the hard heavens. During times of hard heavens, church attendance at many congregations declines. Why is that? It's the result of nasty spiritual climates. We don't understand what's happening to us, so we stay home, watch TV, eat snacks and get fat. Then we come in for prayer on

Sundays saying, "Please pray for me. I had a tough week." Strong flesh and weak spirits characterize that lifestyle. We can't take on Jezebel with weak spirits. Scripture says,

> "And he that overcometh, and keepeth my works unto the end, to him will I give power over the nations" (Revelation 2:26).

Again, the word overcometh means to carry off the victory. You can't go to the nations or even live in peace, for that matter, until you learn how to overcome Ashtoreth and Baal. If you aren't resisting the spiritual climate you live in through prayer and doing the Word, then you are probably being negatively swayed by it. Don't let strong flesh keep you from influencing your territory for Jesus.

WISDOM MADE KNOWN

When you enter new opportunities for advancement, it is important to spiritually discern and to naturally understand the strategies of the Jezebel spirit: how she works in the climate, how she influences the people, how they act when they come under that influence, and how the culture is manipulated by her forces. I knew one pastor who moved to Miami and started a church. Within two years, the church grew to more than 250 people. Then he quit. Why? Jezebel wore him down then took him out through fear, witchcraft, intimidation and a build up of buffeting eunuchs. He didn't even realize what happened to him until after he was gone.

It took me about nine months of walking around in my back yard to understand what was attacking our ministry. No one taught me like I'm teaching you. I was trying to be a nice believer, as I'm sure you are trying to

Jehu exercised his spiritual authority and we must do the same.

be. But even in my own back yard, this spirit got to me and continued to oppress me. It was hard for me to pray. Sometimes I had to travail in prayer to hear from God. I didn't know then like I do now what the spiritual oppression was. I didn't know there was a force trying to keep me out of my destiny. I didn't know that I had to submit to God and spiritually gird myself up to maintain the liberty I had in the Lord (Galatians 5:1). I just tried to pray nice "now-I-lay-me-down-to-sleep" type prayers. But they didn't work. Then I talked to religious people who would pat me on the back and say things like,

"Sonny, everything is going to be alright." No! I'm here to tell you that things are not going to be alright unless you learn to walk in your calling and walk out the Word of God, especially if you want to move forward and make a difference with your life.

Jehu exercised his spiritual authority and we must do the same. This is why God is restoring apostles and prophets to the Body of Christ. We have preached people to sleep with the same old boring sermons. Instead of raising up an army of strong believers, we've raised up a bunch of "peachy keen Christians" devoid of ruthless faith. God is using all five ascension gifts of apostles, prophets, evangelists, pastors and teachers, working together to equip every believer to engage the enemies of our generation (Ephesians 4:12). These equipped believers will not carry a compromising anointing, but a fervency to advance the Gospel of Jesus Christ. They will know how to demonstrate ruthless faith and action in territories where Ashtoreth and Baal are governing. The Bible tells us that it is...

> "God's intent that now through the Church His manifold wisdom might be made known to these rulers and principalities in heavenly places" (Ephesians 3:10).

Paul said,

> "We wrestle not against flesh and blood, but against principalities, against powers, against the rulers of the darkness of this world, against spiritual wickedness in high places" (Ephesians 6:12).

That's who you're wrestling against. The Word of God continues,

> "The weapons of our warfare are not carnal but they are mighty through God, to the pulling down of strongholds" (2 Corinthians 10:4).

Ashtoreth, Jezebel, Ahab and Baal are all demonic strongholds that we, as believers, must breakthrough. How do we breakthrough? Through strong intercessory prayer. It is not easy to pray strong at first. You must develop a fortitude that says, "I'm going to pray no matter how my flesh feels." Most people only want to walk around Jericho the last time. As you attack the hard spiritual climates over your life, the heaviness will start to come off. The areas where you have been weak will become fortified with strength through prayer. And when the Jezebel spirit tries to attack you in those areas, it won't find anything in you and it will not be able to manipulate you anymore. Be just as unyielding and militant in your faith as was Jehu. Draw your spiritual sword and throw away the scabbard. Let that same shiggaown tenacity launch you into victory.

In the next chapter we will discover what a 21st century eunuch looks like and what the Holy Spirit has to say about their fate.

SUMMARY
SHIGGAOWN TENACITY

The word furiously (from the Hebrew word *shiggaown*) meant that Jehu had a militant determination and fierceness about him.

The word overcome (from the Greek word *nikao*) is an interesting word meaning "to carry off the victory."

Jehu demonstrated a ruthless faith in God and carried off the victory.

It takes ruthless faith and militant determination to defeat the Jezebel spirit.

The acts of this apostle of war (Jehu) serve as our blueprint for defeating both Ahab and Jezebel.

God raised up Jehu, an apostle of war, to defeat a goddess of war.

When you enter new opportunities for advancement, it is important to spiritually discern and to naturally understand the strategies of the Jezebel spirit: how she works in the climate, how she influences the people, how they act when they come under that influence, and how the culture is manipulated by her forces.

CHAPTER 9

EUNUCHS OF JEZEBEL

The Holy Spirit is saying, "It's time for the eunuchs of Jezebel to consider their ways." Discover what a 21st century eunuch looks like and why you must guard yourself from becoming Jezebel's wicked assistant.

When Jehu attacked the house of King Ahab to destroy his rule, Jezebel, his wife, painted her face (symbolic of deception) and looked at Jehu through a window. Jehu, a warring apostle, looked up at her, noticed two or three eunuchs standing by, and commanded them to throw the evil queen down (2 Kings 9:30-33). Notice the location of the eunuchs — Jezebel's bedchamber.

The Church is in a time of restoration through reformation, transition, and the establishment of apostolic order. This apostolic order is the prerequisite to the appearing of the glorious Church and the restoration of the tabernacle of David (Ephesians 5:27; Acts 15:16). Before the completion of an apostolic order, however, there are things that can no longer be tolerated in the Church of Jesus Christ, such as:

Enemies, like Tobiah, whom Nehemiah threw out of the house of God because of the ungodly association and position, given him by the priest Eliashib (Nehemiah 13).

Merchandisers such as the Prophet Balaam who was hired to curse Israel (Numbers 22).

The spirit of Jezebel who seduces, deceives, and murders the true prophetic voice.

Eunuchs (the servants) of Jezebel.

The Holy Spirit is not only dealing with the Jezebel spirit, He is also dealing with her eunuchs. Those who refuse to repent are destined for tribulation. Jezebel's eunuchs serve at least 11 functions for their wicked spiritual mother...

1. MESSENGERS OF JEZEBEL

Jezebel uses eunuchs to carry her messages, perform errands, deliver letters, invitations and spread the word. Eunuchs are official couriers and bearers of news. Jezebel prefers to use a eunuch envoy to deliver her message to you rather than coming to you herself.

2. REPRESENTATIVES OF JEZEBEL

Much like sold out Christians are ambassadors for Jesus Christ, eunuchs are authorized as official agents and delegates of Jezebel. And just as we possess certain characteristics of Christ, Jezebel's representatives carry her character and power. When Jezebel can't or doesn't want to attend a meeting herself, look for her eunuch representatives.

3. STUDENTS OF JEZEBEL

Eunuchs are full-time students of Jezebel's teachings. When faced with the truth of Scripture, the eunuch will run to Jezebel for her perverted twist and seducing interpretations.

4. SENTINELS AND GUARDS OF JEZEBEL

Eunuchs watch out for, protect, defend and alert Jezebel of impending harm. Like football players, they block and run interference for those carrying the ball through the defensive line of the opposing team.

5. ATTENDANTS OF JEZEBEL

Eunuchs feel compelled to serve and meet even the most trifling need of Jezebel. They are overly sensitive to her every whim like waiters at a five-star restaurant serving a Head of State.

6. SPIRITUAL CHILDREN OF JEZEBEL

Eunuchs are the spiritual children of Jezebel, oftentimes referring to her as their spiritual mother. Once I gave a ministry assignment to a young man whom I was mentoring in ministry. He told me that he needed permission from his spiritual mother (someone in another city) before he could do what I asked. In a separate incident, a woman told me she had to check with an apostle (of another church) for permission to do what I asked her, even though she was no longer a member of that church. I recognized both of these people as Jezebel's eunuchs and removed them from any leadership training. When you are part of a local church, that set-man is your leader, if not then you need to leave.

7. INTELLIGENCE AGENTS OF JEZEBEL

Eunuchs are Jezebel's intelligence agents who are secretly employed in espionage. Jezebel feeds on knowledge and uses eunuchs as operatives to gather vital information to maintain her control and influence. Many times I have seen her spies snooping for information that was none of their business.

8. DEVOTED TO JEZEBEL'S WELLBEING

Eunuchs have a misplaced devotion, commitment and loyalty to the purposes of Jezebel. They offer themselves freely with time and attention to her wellbeing. They are strongly attached, zealous and devoted admirers of her. The word devote is from the Latin word *devovere* (de + vovere) meaning to vow. Thus, the devoted eunuch is one set apart, consecrated and dedicated to Jezebel.

9. ARMOR BEARERS TO JEZEBEL

Jezebel's eunuch is an armorbearer. Like a squire that carries the armor of a knight, Jezebel's eunuchs are always by her side carrying her armor and weapons.

10. WITHOUT SPIRITUAL STRENGTH

Eunuchs are those castrated by the spirit of Jezebel. The Hebrew word for eunuch (*cariyc*) represents a castrated person and keeper of the bedchamber (chamberlain). This lack of spiritual strength is what allows Jezebel to draw the eunuch to begin with — and is what makes it so difficult for the eunuch to break free even upon revelation of the truth.

My father purchased a fine looking stallion when I was a young man and my job was to take care of him. He was a magnificent Dutch Warmblood, quite valuable, with a strong back, hindquarters, and incredibly powerful. When we built the barn and horse stalls, the one prepared for the stallion had to be fortified because he had the strength to tear it apart at will.

Unlike a dossal gilded horse that could be led around with a simple lead rope snapped to an eye-ring on a halter, this stallion required two chain leads wrapped solidly around his nose to walk him around.

Like this stallion, God wants His children spiritually strong, full of His power and might. Jezebels' eunuchs, however, are weak spiritually and dependant on her warring abilities. They are made completely reliant on her.

11. KEEPERS OF JEZEBEL'S BED

As chamberlains, Jezebel's eunuchs are allowed unrestricted access into her private dwelling. One's bedroom is the most private and intimate place in the home. Such access represents the intimate relationship the eunuch has with Jezebel.

The Spirit of God offers the same admonishment for both Jezebel and her eunuchs alike — repent. Scripture declares,

> "I gave her space to repent of her fornication" (Revelation 2:21).

How long was that space? Only the Spirit of God knows that answer.

Like Jehu of old, my instruction to the eunuch is, "Consider your ways; stop serving Jezebel and throw her out of your life." If you have been a eunuch, it's time to ask Jesus for His forgiveness. The Word of God says,

> "If we confess our sins, he is faithful and just to forgive us our sins, and to cleanse us from all unrighteousness" (1 John 1:9).

SARAH GETS FREE FROM
PHYLLIS' CONTROL

Eunuchs can break free from Jezebel and some do. One Sunday at church Sarah had an incredible experience at the altar. The Holy Spirit opened her eyes to the deceit, control and manipulation that Phyllis had used to keep her isolated from others who could speak into her life. It was so dramatic that it was almost as though she had put Phyllis in the place of Jesus Himself. But now her eyes were opened. It was clear to her that she had to break free of Phyllis's influence.

She confronted Phyllis and told her that she could no longer attend her Bible studies, and wanted to break away from their relationship. Phyllis was angry and told Sarah that she would be in great danger to do so. But it was too late for those types of false prophetic warnings. Sarah was determined to be free.

Sarah saw Phyllis in the grocery store about a year after she left the group. Sarah could still feel the spiritual pull from Phyllis. Today Sarah is still overcoming the time that she spent being deceived by the Jezebel spirit. The group broke up, but Sarah reports that Phyllis is still hopping from church to church looking for others who will feed at her table.

Scripture is very clear regarding those who refuse to repent of operating with a Jezebel spirit,

> "Behold, I will cast her into a bed, and them that commit adultery with her into great tribulation, except they repent of their deeds" (Revelation 2:22).

This decree of tribulation by Jesus, our Chief Apostle, was not only directed to those operating by a Jezebel spirit, but also to those who "commit adultery with her" — her eunuchs. The word tribulation *(thlipsis)* means the application of continuous pressure without relief from stress, grievance and trouble. The common stress and pressure from modern life is nothing compared to the pressure (thlipsis) the Holy Spirit allows on the unrepentant eunuchs of Jezebel; it is pressure without relief.

I WILL KILL HER CHILDREN

> "And I will kill her children with death; and all the churches shall know that I am he which searcheth the reins and hearts: and I will give unto every one of you according to your works" (Revelation 2:23).

"To kill her children" means anything that Jezebel gives birth to in her ministry will not stand and will be cut off by the Lord.

In the next chapter we will review some key points we have learned about Jezebel and her slavery and how to break free from her control.

SUMMARY
EUNUCHS OF JEZEBEL

Notice the location of the eunuchs — Jezebel's bedchamber.

The word tribulation *(thlipsis)* means the application of continuous pressure without relief from stress, grievance and trouble.

Jezebel uses eunuchs to carry her messages, perform errands, deliver letters, invitations and spread the word.

Eunuchs are authorized as official agents and delegates of Jezebel.

Eunuchs are full-time students of the teachings of Jezebel.

Eunuchs feel compelled to serve and meet even the most trifling need of Jezebel.

Jezebel feeds on knowledge and uses eunuchs as operatives to gather vital information to maintain her control and influence.

Eunuchs are those castrated by the spirit of Jezebel.

As chamberlains, Jezebel's eunuchs are allowed unrestricted access into her private dwelling.

CHAPTER 10

GOD'S ABOLITIONIST MOVEMENT

Bondage to the Jezebel spirit is an evil form of slavery. Every believer should aggressively stand against this usurper of liberty and join God's abolitionist movement.

The Jezebel spirit has battled God's people throughout the ages: Delilah seduced Samson in an attempt to discover his great strength and use it against him (Judges 16:5). The Philistines cut off King Saul's head and displayed his armor like a trophy in the house of Ashtaroth after he committed suicide (1 Samuel 21:9-10). King David lusted after Bathsheba (2 Samuel 11:2). Solomon became prey to Ashtoreth, the goddess of the Sidonians (1 Kings 11:5). God's prophets have been warning Jehova's people about this wicked spirit for generations, too. The Prophet Samuel warned the people to put away Ashtaroth and serve the Lord only (1 Samuel 7:3-4). Prophet Jeremiah challenged the worship of the Queen of Heaven (Jeremiah 44) and Jesus, the Prophet, warned the church in Thyatira about the dangers of Jezebel (Revelation 2:20-22).

You've been duly warned and you have everything you need to war. The Word of God is replete with truth that enables us to defeat the Jezebel spirit every time. Through prayer, the application of God's Word and the knowledge that you have gained through reading this book you can overcome the Jezebel spirit. Let's review some final thoughts helpful in overcoming the Jezebel spirit.

THE HIJACKER

Jezebel wants to usurp your authority, get you to seek her approval, separate you from others and contract her services. Never give in to Jezebels attempt to usurp your authority.

To usurp means to seize without permission or legal authority the power or rights of another through force, coercion, bullying, intimidation, deception or manipulation. The word hijack probably captures the fundamental nature of the

Jezebel spirit better than any word in the English vocabulary.

On American Airlines flight 969 departing Miami, Fla. to Managua, Nicaragua, the lines for ticketing and boarding passes were several city blocks long. I was with a team heading to Central America for a national Gospel meeting. We had arrived two hours early for our international flight and still weren't confident that it was enough time to get through check-in and security screening. Central American flights are known to be loaded to capacity with travelers packing newly purchased items in their suitcases. While we were waiting in line a woman traveling with two companions unlocked the vinyl straps that organized us into nice rows like cattle in shoots. Then without saying a single word she bypassed everyone in line with her company , fully loaded with luggage on three pushcarts.

When I saw the boldness of this woman to cut line in front of so many people I recognized it as a striking example of the Jezebel spirit. Her unwillingness to go to the end of the line the way every child is taught in elementary school demonstrated the Jezebel spirit's eagerness to hijack an unearned position. Not only were her actions rude but they captured a natural example of a spiritual truth: Jezebel will usurp positions that don't belong to her.

JEZEBEL'S CONSENT

Don't seek Jezebel's approval.

Many former Jezebel eunuchs have told me that during their process of breaking free from her control they still felt an urge to seek Jezebel's approval for their decisions. If you have the same feelings, remember this: You don't need Jezebel's approval to make decisions or move on with your life. Stop talking to her! You don't need Jezebel to be your teacher, prophetess, mentor, advisor, confidant or friend. Nor should you feed her any information about your life. Cut the information flow off and avoid her seducing flattery at all cost. Learn the weapons of your warfare against this spirit: the Word of God, the blood of Jesus, your testimony, submission to godly authority in a Spirit-filled church, prayer, and your will. Say, "No!" to Jezebel's activity and mean it.

AVOID SEGREGATION

Don't let the Jezebel spirit detach you from others.

At one time the telephone company had a monopoly on telephone service. The lack of competition and exclusive control gave them unmitigated power over their customers.

One can only imagine the potential for corruption when there are many buyers and only one seller.

Like corporate monopolies, Jezebel desires unlimited control over her eunuchs. Jezebel doesn't approve of free public access to her neophytes. To reinforce her controls, Jezebel screens outside thoughts and opinions and limits access to her victims through isolation.

You don't have to battle Jezebel alone. Plug into a good local church and use God's Word as your ultimate guide. Make friends with other people outside Jezebel's circle of influence. Submission to the right authority offers a great wall of protection. Stand your ground in your rightful position. Take your will away from Jezebel, submit yourself to God and let His Word govern your life and actions.

CANCEL JEZEBEL'S CONTRACT SERVICES

Don't ask Jezebel to do anything for you.

If Jezebel has been controlling you, then you may not be used to making your own decisions without her consent, interacting with others outside her influence or handling uncomfortable problems on your own. This makes you vulnerable to Jezebel's offer of help. Jezebel likes to offer contract employment services. Stay away from Jezebel's flattery, seductions and offers to handle anything for you.

AN ABOLITIONIST

Join the cause and become an abolitionist against the Jezebel spirit.

Bondage to the Jezebel spirit is a form of slavery. Every believer should aggressively stand against this usurper of liberty.

A portrait of John Brown hangs at the National Portrait Gallery in Washington, D.C. John Brown was a well-known abolitionist who opposed the injustice of slavery. He was hanged in 1859 for attacking a federal armory at Harpers Ferry, Va. that lead to the genesis of the Civil War. I like what Frederick Douglass, the most prominent African-American of his time, wrote about Brown's determiniation to fight tyranny: "Did John Brown fail? John Brown began the war that ended American slavery and made this a free Republic. His zeal in the cause of my race was far greater than mine. I could live for the slave, but he could die for him."

Douglass captures the spirit needed to free those overcome by the Jezebel spirit — "zeal in the cause." Jesus has set us free from every bondage. Join God's abolitionist movement and declare independence today from the Jezebel spirit.

SUMMARY
GOD'S ABOLITIONIST MOVEMENT

Jezebel wants to usurp your authority, get you to seek her approval, separate you from others and contract her services.

To usurp means to seize without permission or legal authority the power or rights of another through force, coercion, bullying, intimidation, deception or manipulation.

The word hijack probably captures the essence of the Jezebel spirit better than any word in the English vocabulary.

You don't need Jezebel's approval to make decisions or move on with your life.

Jezebel doesn't approve of free public access to her neophytes.

To reinforce her controls, Jezebel screens outside thoughts and opinions and limits access to her victims through isolation.

Make friends with other people outside Jezebel's circle of influence.

Stay away from Jezebel's flattery, seductions and offers to handle anything for you.

WHEN THERE IS NO REPENTENCE

If you recognize the evil tendencies of the Jezebel spirit in yourself, then repent. If we confess our sin to God, He is faithful and just to forgive our sin and cleanse us from all unrighteousness with the blood of Jesus (1 John 1:7-9). I can't stress this enough. Time is running out for the Jezebel spirit. With an army of believers rising up with knowledge of her wiles and the discernment to recognize this spirit's many faces, those who yield their wills to the Jezebel spirit may soon find themselves on a bed of tribulation. Scripture declares,

> "And I gave her space to repent of her fornication; and she repented not. Behold, I will cast her into a bed, and them

that commit adultery with her into great tribulation, except they repent of their deeds" (Revelation 2:21-22).

God gave Queen Jezebel space to repent of her fornication and she refused. We can read about her shameful fate in the Bible. The word fornication is the Greek word "porneia," meaning illicit sexual intercourse, worship of idols, and intercourse with idols. Control can be an idol, and operating in control is a sin. Our lives are not our own. The Holy Spirit, not the Jezebel spirit, should control our lives.

This is a serious matter. Remember, because Jezebel and her companions refused to repent, God "cast them into a bed of tribulation." God is saying that people — men or women — who tap into and carry the controlling, manipulative Jezebel spirit will have miserable lives filled with nothing but trouble. That miserable trouble is called tribulation.

Understand that you may have hurts and wounds that made you vulnerable to carrying this spirit. Ask God for emotional healing and deliverance. Also know that control, fear and rejection are closely related. Those who are controlling often become that way because they are scared of getting taken advantage of or being hurt and rejected.

Our God is not going to do a work that nobody knows about. The whole Church is going to know that God handled Jezebel. Repent now and turn from control. There is life for those with Jezebel spirits who repent. Be a living testimony to the blood of Jesus and then help others get free, too!

INDEX

D

Emotional bonding 22
Emotional healing 192
Emotional hurts 7
Enemies 172
Enemy 8
Engage the enemies 166
Enslave 9
Entice 51,129
Environment 37
Environmental activist 81
Envy 120
Ephesus 159
Equip every believer 166
Erotic lust 80
Error 9
Espionage 175
Establishment 171
Eunuch 38
Eunuchs 11,30,147,172,179
Evangelistic ministry 8
Evil agenda 5
Evil tendencies 191
Exalted one 139
Examples of spiritual truths
        147
Example of the Jezebel spirit
        185
Exercising authority 166
Exhort 47
Exploit 7
Expose 8
Expressly 48

F

Fainthearted 7
Faith 23
False accusations 12,124
False authority 33
False god 81
False government 139,150
False manifestations 90
False personal prophecy 51
False prophecy 15,43,144
False prophetesses 6
False prophetic insight 51
False sense of security 91
False signs and wonders 89
False tears 11
Fame 56
Familiar spirits 51
Family 61
Family inheritance 129
Family members 65
Famine 136
Fantasy 81,126
Fasting 69
Faults 22
Fear 11,165,192
Fear's message 105
Fearful message 69
Feed 7,178,186
Feelings 158
Female deity 82
Feminist goddess movement
        82

INVITATION TO DESTINY

Are you hungry for more of God? In addition to preaching the Gospel around the world, we also pastor a powerful, Spirit-filled church in South Florida. The Spirit of God told us to build a church from which to send forth believers that could reach their cities and impact the nations for Jesus Christ.

Have you been searching for God only to find religion? Spirit of Life Ministries (SOLM) is a multi-cultural church where all races gather together in unity and cares for the needs of the whole family. Is something missing from your life? SOLM is a church where you can receive what you need from the Lord. We believe in divine healing, manifesting the gifts of the Spirit, prayer results, miracles, prosperity, finding purpose and making a difference. With God all things are possible.

Are you looking for a place to grow? SOLM is a new apostolic church with all five-fold ministry gifts operating. We have a prophetic call and mandate to equip, activate and release every believer into the work of the ministry according to Ephesians 4:11-12. We invite you to come and connect with your destiny and receive confirmation, impartation and activation for your life.

Come adventure with us,
Jonas and Rhonda Clark

SPIRIT OF LIFE MINISTRIES WORLD HEADQUARTERS
27 WEST HALLANDALE BEACH BLVD. • HALLANDALE BEACH, FLA. 33009
800.943.6490 • WWW.JONASCLARK.COM

Want to know more about how to overcome
spiritual enemies, like Jezebel?

Find answers in THE VOICE® magazine.

Sign up to receive a
FREE Issue of THE VOICE® magazine
at www.thevoicemagazine.com

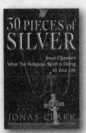

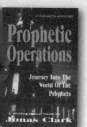

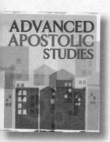

Dominion • Authority • Purpose

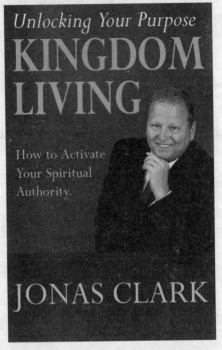

ISBN 978-1-886885-21-4 - HardCover

Are you experiencing Kingdom Living?

Jonas' latest work shows you how to activate your kingship and live the life of purpose, authority and dominion that belongs you in Christ.

Kingdom Living offers practical insights into what Jesus meant when He said, "It is the Father's good pleasure to give unto you the Kingdom." This book unlocks mysteries of the Kingdom for your life. When you read Kingdom Living you will discover how to tap into the power of the Kingdom of God in you and how to pray the way Jesus prayed.

Kingdom Living equips you with action steps designed to help you experience what the Bible says about restoration, dominion, spiritual authority -- and your role in the Kingdom of God.

To order, log on to www.JonasClark.com
or call 800.943.6490.